COLLABORATIONS:
ENGLISH IN OUR LIVES

Intermediate 2 Teacher's Edition

The publication of *Collaborations* was directed by the members of the Heinle & Heinle Secondary and Adult ESL Publishing Team:

Editorial Director: Roseanne Mendoza
Senior Production Services Coordinator: Lisa McLaughlin
Market Development Director: Jonathan Boggs

Also participating in the publication of the program were:

Vice President and Publisher, ESL: Stanley Galek
Managing Developmental Editor, ESL: Amy Lawler
Senior Assistant Editor: Sally Conover
Production Editor: Maryellen Killeen
Manufacturing Coordinator: Mary Beth Hennebury
Full Service Design and Production: PC&F, Inc.
Illustration Program: G. Brian Karas and PC&F, Inc.

Manufactured in the United States of America.

ISBN: 0-8384-6643-5

Heinle & Heinle is a division of International Thomson Publishing, Inc.

Photo Credits

The following credits refer to photos and text appearing in the student book.

Cover: David Moss, top; Jean Bernard, center left; Corpus Christi Literacy Council, center middle; Thai-Hung Pham Nguyen, center right; © Jonathan Stark/Heinle & Heinle Publishers, bottom.

Unit 1: Jean Bernard, 1, 4 bottom, 5, 6, 8, 9 left and top right, 13 bottom left; Mike Johnson, 2, 4 top; Mariano Ramos Hernandez (book cover), 7; Peter Lee, 9 middle right; © Jonathan Stark/Heinle & Heinle Publishers, 9; Ulli Stetzler, 13; David Moss, 15.

Unit 2: Jeanne H. Schmedlen, 19, 20, 21, 23, 24; Thai-Hung Pham Nguyen, 25; Corpus Christi Literacy Council, 26, 32.

Unit 3: David Moss, 35, 36, 38, 40, 42, 45 top, 47 bottom; Jean Bernard, 45 bottom; Marie H. Bias, 47 top.

Unit 4: Greater Corpus Christi Business Alliance, 51; Corpus Christi Literacy Council, 52; AP/Wide World Photos, 53; Betty Lynch, 56, 57, 58; © King Photography/FPG, 62 top; © C. Peter Borsari/FPG, 62 bottom; © Kozlowski Productions/FPG, 63; © Jonathan Stark/Heinle & Heinle Publishers, 65.

Unit 5: David Moss, 69 right and bottom, 70, 71, 73, 77 left, 78, 79; © Alan McGee/FPG, 69 left bottom; © Jonathan Stark/Heinle & Heinle Publishers, 76; Marie H. Bias, 77 right.

Unit 6: Jean Bernard, 85, 86, 87, 88, 90, 91, 92, 93, 94, 95, 96; Tsekyi Dolma, 98; Donna Carroll, 85.

Text Credits:

Unit 4: Stevie Wonder, excerpt from "Living for the City." Copyright © 1973. Published by Jobete Music Co., Inc./Black Bull Music. Reprinted by permission of Jobete Music Co., Inc., Los Angeles, CA., 62; Lyrics from "Sixteen Tons," copyright © Warner/Chappel, Los Angeles, CA., 63.

Unit 5: Gallup Poll, source: U.S. Immigration and Naturalization Service, 75.

COLLABORATIONS:
ENGLISH IN OUR LIVES

Intermediate 2 Teacher's Edition

Jean Bernard
Donna Moss
Lynda Terrill

Heinle & Heinle Publishers
A Division of International Thomson Publishing, Inc.
Boston, MA 02116, U.S.A.

   The ITP logo is a trademark under license.

CONTENTS

*Glossary of Grammatical Terms and a List of Commo

Language Structures	Higher Order Skills and Strategies	Community Building in the Classroom
• pronoun referents • subject complements • relative clauses • preposition clusters	• previewing a reading by asking questions and reading captions • interpreting metaphors • reading graphs • reading editorials • connecting one's life experience to a text • reflective writing on the unit themes	• learning about each others accomplishments and talents • sharing ideas on maintaining cultural traditions in North America • conducting a community survey • planning a cultural event
• past perfect • past perfect continuous • root words and affixes	• previewing a reading by asking questions • paraphrasing a reading • comparing • paraphrasing idioms • identifying and using similes and metaphors • scanning for specific information • skimming for general information • connecting one's life experience to the text • reflective writing on the unit themes	• learning about each others learning strategies • comparing cultures • sharing information about educational opportunities • learning about each other's educational and employment history
• reported speech • direct quotations • advice with *should* and *ought to*	• previewing a reading by answering questions • reacting to poetry • interpreting poetry • writing poetry • identifying problems, solutions and consequences • connecting one's life experience to a text • reflective writing on the unit themes	• sharing customs of engagements and weddings • comparing cultural differences in dating and marriage • brainstorming solutions to problems
• indirect questions • forming hyphenated words	• identifying short-term and long-term goals • writing an outline for an oral presentation • making an oral presentation • using mood, rhythm to understand meaning of literature • connecting one's life experience to a text • reflective writing on the unit themes	• practicing job interview questions • sharing information about job opportunities and job skills • finding and using community resources • comparing short-term and long-term goals
• obligation with *must* and *have to* • requests with *would, could, can,* and *will*	• previewing a reading and answering questions • writing questions about a reading passage • summarizing a story • retelling a story • reading bar graphs and tables • making an oral presentation • connecting one's life experience to a text • reflective writing on the unit themes	• sharing experiences as new arrivals in North America • developing a survey • sharing results of interviews • sharing research information
• conditionals with past possibilities • conditionals with future possibilities • *wish* with past plural verbs	• previewing a reading by using visuals • sequencing chronological events • scanning for specific information • creating timelines • prewriting by note taking • connecting one's own experience with the text • reflective writing on the unit themes	• learning about other's prospects for the future • learning about major events in others' lives • sharing news from home • sharing information from a travel agency

regular Verbs appear on pages 103 through 105.

THE WORLD

Do you want to see where the people in this book come from? Their countries are labeled.

Canada

Pacific Ocean

United States

Atlantic Ocean

Puerto Rico

Venezuela

Equator · · · · · · · · · · · · · Colombia

Peru

Bolivia

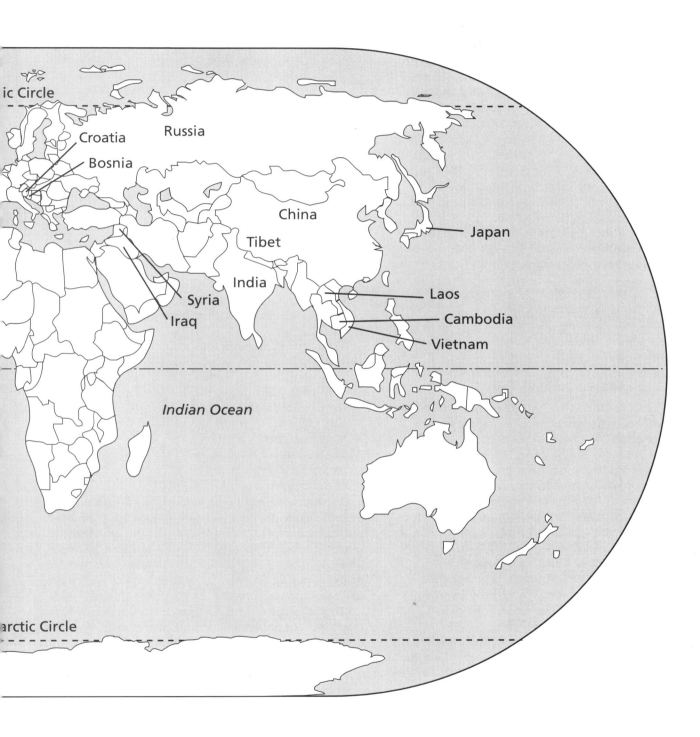

ic Circle

Croatia

Bosnia

Russia

China

Tibet

Japan

India

Syria

Iraq

Laos

Cambodia

Vietnam

Indian Ocean

arctic Circle

ABOUT THIS SERIES

Our purpose for creating this series is to provide opportunities for adult immigrants and refugees to develop English language and literacy skills while reflecting, as individuals and with others, on their changing lives.

We believe that the best adult ESL classrooms are places where learners and teachers work collaboratively, talk about issues that matter to them, use compelling materials, and engage in tasks that reflect their life experiences and concerns. We see learning as a process in which students are encouraged to participate actively, and the classroom as a place where students share and reflect on their experiences and rehearse for new roles in the English-speaking world beyond its walls.

How are the books in the series organized?

Unlike most adult ESL materials, *Collaborations* is not organized around linguistic skills nor life skill competencies, but around contexts for language use in learners' lives. Each student book consists of six units, beginning with the individual and moving out through the series of ever-widening language environments shown below.

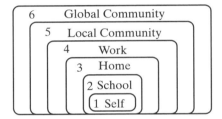

The units revolve around the narratives of newcomers who tell or write of their experiences. Each unit focuses on a particular site in North America, generally one that has a significant number of ESL programs and learners. In some locations, we have chosen a particular ethnic group. In others, we have made the multi-ethnic character of the area the focal point of the unit. It is our belief that within the marvelous diversity of newcomers, there are seeds for finding similarities—the common threads of experience—as newcomers make sense of managing life in a new setting with new constraints as well as new possibilities.

Grammar, vocabulary development, language functions, and competencies are interwoven throughout the units in each student book. However, the organizing principles are reversed from those of most traditional materials. Rather than selecting linguistic items and then creating contexts to elicit them, *Collaborations* addresses language development and competencies as they naturally emerge from the contexts and the authentic texts. For those who wish to focus more on specific competencies or language structures, detailed indexes are provided to enable participants to identify where the item is taught, and where resources for further practice can be found.

Collaborations is intended for use with learners of English in adult programs in school districts, community colleges, and community-based programs. While it is an excellent fit in non-credit programs, it may also be the right choice for some credit programs because of its strong emphasis on critical thinking and problem solving. The assessment component for the program—with its placement guidelines and instructions for portfolio assessment as well as more formal quizzes and tests—facilitates adaptation to either program. Particularly at the higher levels of the program, there is an emphasis on development of skills needed in academic programs, GED study, and workplace situations.

What are the other components of *Collaborations*?

The supplementary **workbook** for each level is correlated to the student book. It offers independent study tasks that recycle and reinforce language points from the corresponding units of the student book. Each workbook unit has a predictable structure that contains the following:
- grammar work in context
- extended reading and writing
- vocabulary work
- competency-based tasks
- tests and self assessment

In each unit, the workbook tasks follow the sequence of the activities in the student book and further develop the unit themes.

The **teacher's resource kit** consists of a variety of materials to extend classroom activities and to facilitate and assess learners' progress. The materials listed below are provided in a format that can be inserted into the teacher's kit binder.
- the teacher's edition
- wall maps of the world and of North America
- blackline activity masters
- the assessment program
- overhead transparencies
- cassette tape

The teacher's edition includes reduced student book pages, suggestions from the authors, insights from field test instructors who used the material in their classes, and space for teachers to keep their own teaching/learning journals. The transparencies are intended to be used for problem-posing activities, Language Experience writing, and oral language practice, among other things.

The assessment program includes traditional benchmarks such as pre-tests, individual unit checks, midterm and final exams, as well as guidelines for developing learner portfolios. The program is meant to encourage learners to set their own goals and monitor their own progress.

Finally, there is a cassette tape for each level. The student tape contains all the stories from each unit of the student book as well as an authentic "review interview," for which there is an accompanying worksheet in the Activity Masters in the teacher's kit.

Each unit in the student book is designed to provide at least 10 hours of activities, or 60 hours for the entire book.

However, if used in conjunction with the workbook and teacher's kit, each unit provides at least 16 hours of activities for a total of 96 hours.

ABOUT THIS LEVEL

What is included in each unit?

Each unit in this level includes:

- an introduction to the geographic area where stories in the unit are based.
- authentic narratives and photographs that have been collected from immigrant and migrant communities throughout North America. At this level, poetry, newspaper editorials, songs, folk tales, and proverbs from around the world are also included.
- multiple opportunities to react/respond to these texts and to relate them to personal experience.
- an invitation to take a closer look at the way language is used in the opening story by *Playing with Story Language.*
- guided practice in pre-GED reading and academic learning strategies in/through participation in *Think It Over* tasks, which engage learners in reacting to more formal, non-narrative writing, often accompanied by graphs, charts, or illustrations.
- one or more interactive *Learning About Each Other* tasks to foster fluency while building community among learners in the classroom.
- *Doing It in English* tasks, in which learners practice functions of English for purposes appropriate to each context.
- *Sharing Experiences* and *Sharing Ideas* activities, which invite learners to contribute their own unique perspectives on unit themes as they practice new language and critical thinking skills, such as recognizing figures of speech and identifying learning strategies.
- an invitation to *Journal Writing*, which allows students to react in writing to the themes of the unit and interact on paper with the teacher. At this level, learners are offered several options or choices of topic.
- *Other Voices from North America* which offer learners a chance to expand their reading experience by encountering a wide variety of narratives as well as other writings of varying lengths and styles.
- *Reading Strategy* and *Learning Strategy* boxes which highlight useful study strategies and bring them to conscious awareness.
- *Country Information* boxes which present informational profiles of the countries or territories represented in the unit.
- a focus on *Ideas for Action* in which learners reflect critically on their situations and decide together how they can empower themselves.
- a plan for *Bringing the Outside In*, so that learners may gain new experience and knowledge from resource people, printed materials, or realia brought in from outside the classroom.
- a list of *Options for Learning*, in which individual learners choose to study one or more communicative skills from a list of competencies (and follow up with activity worksheets).
- an opportunity to *Look Back*, where learners reflect on what they have learned, what they want to study more about, and which activities suit them the most.
- a *Checklist for Learning* to provide learners with a way to monitor their own progress and to review previous material.

QUESTIONS ABOUT COLLABORATIONS

The language in this book is not as controlled as other materials I've used. Will this be too difficult for my students?

Adults have been learning languages, with and without language instruction, from the time of the first human migration. Students in an English-language setting acquire language most efficiently when there is something worth communicating about. When the building blocks of language are made accessible, acquisition becomes natural and pleasurable. The aim in this series is to provide learners with the tools they need and to create conditions in which communicating is well worth the effort. Because language is a medium for negotiating social relationships, part of the goal is to create a classroom community in which English takes on meaning and purpose. The obstacles learners face because of their incomplete mastery of the English in the material are more than offset by compelling reasons to communicate.

What should I do if my students do not yet know the grammar or vocabulary in the stories and tasks?

Any teacher who has ever faced a class of eager ESL learners has had to grapple with the reality that learners come with differences in their prior exposure to English and with their own individual language-learning timetables, strategies, and abilities. There is no syllabus which will address directly and perfectly the stage of language development of any particular learner, let alone a diverse group. This material reflects the belief that learners can benefit most when forms and functions are made available in the service of authentic communicative tasks. Teaching is most effective when it taps into areas that are ready for development.

For this reason, tasks in *Collaborations* are open-ended and multi-faceted, allowing individuals to make progress according to their current stages of development. The inclusion of numerous collaborative tasks makes it possible for more capable peers as well as instructors to provide assistance to learners as they move to new stages of growth in mastering English.

It is not necessary for learners to understand every word or grammatical structure in order to respond to a story, theme, or issue. The context created by evocative photographs, by familiar situations, and by predictable tasks usually allows learners to make good guesses about meaning even when they do not control all of the vocabulary or structures they see. Any given reading or activity is successful if it evokes a reaction in the learner, and if it creates a situation in which learners are eager to respond. When appropriate language structures and vocabulary are provided toward that end, language acquisition is facilitated. Within this framework, total mastery is not critical: total engagement is.

What do I do about errors my students make?

Errors are a natural part of the language-learning process, as learners test out their hypotheses about how the new language works. Different learners benefit from varying degrees of attention to form and function. For this reason, there are supplementary activities in the workbooks and teacher's kits where learners can give focused attention to vocabulary, grammar, functions, and competencies. The detailed indexes can also assist users in locating language forms that are of immediate concern to them. Form-focused activities can be used as material for explicit study or practice, as well as for monitoring progress in language development. This series operates on the assumption that the most important ingredient for language acquisition is the opportunity to use English to communicate about things that matter. The supplementary materials will be most effective if the time set aside to focus on form is not seen as an end in and of itself, but rather, is viewed as a necessary component in developing the tools for meaningful communication and classroom community-building.

ACKNOWLEDGMENTS

This book would never have been possible without the enthusiastic help of those whose stories grace these pages. We cannot thank them all by name here, but their names appear with their stories. We are grateful to colleagues, teachers, and administrators who helped so much in arranging interviews and collecting stories.

We gratefully acknowledge the originators of this series, Gail Weinstein-Shr and Jann Huizenga, as well as the other members of the original "think tank," whose ideas have continued to inspire and shape our work. We are indebted to our reviewers for their valuable insights, and to the field testers for sharing their experiences with us. We are also grateful to our mutual friend, Miriam Burt, for bringing us together.

At Heinle & Heinle, the authors are grateful to the Collaborations team. We'd also like to thank PC&F for their expert editing and production work.

We also gratefully acknowledge our sponsoring organizations, our families, and our friends for their enthusiastic and continued support.

ABOUT THE TEACHER'S EDITION

There are four components to the **Teacher's Edition.** First, on each two-page spread, there is a reduced image of the **Student Book pages** for easy visual reference. Second, in a column titled **Authors' Notes,** we have included our own comments, in which we: explain our purpose for designing a particular activity, provide ideas on how to carry it out, or suggest variations for expansion and modification to accommodate different levels and learning styles. Third, in **Field Testers' Notes,** found in an adjacent column, accounts are provided from colleagues around the country who have had an opportunity to use this material. Fourth, and most importantly in our view, we have included an **Instructor's Journal,** the purpose of which is to provide space to document successes and excitements, disappointments and challenges, as well as insights or hunches about what is happening with particular learners. We believe that reflections on individual classrooms are often the best source of information for future teaching. It is our hope that these logs will be shared with colleagues, leading toward the creation of communities of teacher and learners who support one another in their important and challenging work.

Unit 1

Maintaining Cultural Traditions in Connecticut

Located in New England, Connecticut is a small state with a population of about 3,300,000. The majority of people who live and work in Connecticut were born outside of the mainland United States. Connecticut is well known for its manufacturing and service industries, where most of the newcomers to the state find jobs. The main story in this unit is from Waterbury, a major urban center with a large Puerto Rican community. Well known for its metal and rubber industries, Waterbury was once called "The Brass Capital of the World." Other major cities in Connecticut include New Haven and Hartford.

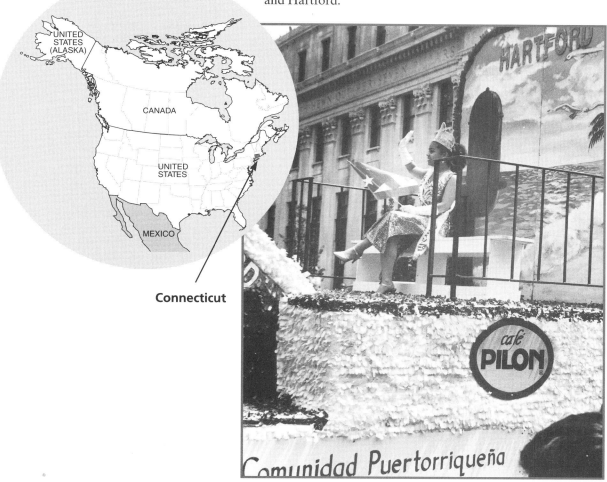

Connecticut

Mariano Ramos Hernandez' Story

A. Look at the photograph of Mariano Ramos Hernandez and read the caption. Where is he from? What kind of work does he do? What other things do you want to know about him? Write three questions.

Mariano Ramos Hernandez is president of the Puerto Rican Poets' Society in Waterbury, Connecticut. He has published two books, and has received many awards for his poetry. He lives in Waterbury with his wife, Alma.

B. Read the story.
Keep your questions in mind as you read.

I write about everything, but the most important thing for me is my homeland, Puerto Rico. My first poem was published when I was just eight years old. It was a very short poem called "The Tree." A couple of years later, I wrote another one for my best friend, a girl who went to school with me. It was called "Celinda." After that, every time I fell in love with a girl I wrote a poem to her.

I first left Puerto Rico in 1949. I was only a kid. I came to work on a farm in New Jersey for 50 cents an hour. Since then, I've had lots of jobs—I've been a hospital worker, a bus boy, a waiter, and a cook. I call myself a lucky guy. I always live the way you see me now—poor and humble, but happy.

I've worked hard for the last 39 years. Sometimes I had three jobs at once, but I never stopped writing poems. I used to stay up until one or two o'clock in the morning, just writing. Now that I'm retired, I have more time. They call me "El Bardo Del Vivi," (the poet of the Vivi) after a river that flows through my hometown of Utuado in central Puerto Rico. All of my poetry goes back to that place.

I am an original. I like my poetry to be understood, even by people who have no education at all, because in my poems I give a message. The only way to make that message clear is to use original words.

We Puerto Ricans are also Americans, but we want to maintain our culture here in Connecticut. We do it by speaking our language, writing books in Spanish, dancing, and organizing events like Three Kings' Day and the Puerto Rican Parade. People put out their flags and wear straw hats to show we are proud of being who we are. Our community has been doing things like this for a long time. As a matter of fact, other groups have followed our example.

IDIOMS
fall in love
only a kid
a lucky guy

How long has it been since you left your homeland?
Do you consider yourself a lucky person? Explain why or why not.
How do you maintain cultural traditions in North America?

Playing with Story Language

A. Listen to the first paragraph again. Fill in the missing words.

> _____ write about everything, but the most important thing for _____ is _____ homeland, Puerto Rico. _____ first poem was published when _____ was eight years old. It was in a Puerto Rican magazine, a very short poem called "The Tree." A couple of years later, _____ wrote another poem for _____ best friend, a girl who went to school with _____. It was called "Celinda." After that, every time _____ fell in love with a girl _____ wrote a poem to her.

B. Rewrite the same paragraph so that it is *about* Mariano Ramos. Follow the example of the first sentence.

He writes about everything, but the most important thing for him is his
homeland, Puerto Rico.
_____
_____
_____
_____

C. Work with a partner. Take turns reading these parts of Mariano's story aloud. Pay special attention to the highlighted words. These words stand for other words or numbers in the same group of sentences. Write what the words stand for in the blanks to the right.

1. I first left Puerto Rico in 1949. I was only a kid. I came to work on a farm for 50 cents an hour. Since **then**, I've had lots of jobs. _____

2. They call me "El Bardo Del Vivi," after a river that flows through my hometown of Utuado in central Puerto Rico. All of my poetry goes back to **that place**. _____

3. We want to maintain our culture here in Connecticut. We do **it** _____ by speaking **our language**, writing books in Spanish, dancing, and organizing events like Three Kings' Day and the Puerto Rican Parade.

INSTRUCTOR'S JOURNAL

_____
_____
_____
_____
_____
_____
_____
_____

Page 2   Correlates with:
Transparency: page 1
Audiotape: Story on tape

AUTHORS' NOTES • • •

1 The stories in this unit reflect the individual perspectives of longer term immigrants, and focus on strategies they have used to adapt to life in North America while maintaining their own cultural identities. Before introducing Mariano Ramos Hernandez' story, you might want to have learners turn to the opening page and read the factual information about Connecticut. Ask them to describe the scene in the photograph. What clues in the picture help them guess who the woman is and what she is doing? How does the photo relate to the unit title?

As students look at the photo (or transparency) of Mariano Ramos Hernandez on page 2, you could tell them that he first left Puerto Rico in 1949. In what ways do they think he has changed? In what ways has he remained the same?

A. To help orient your students to the concept of poetry, you might introduce a popular poem as did Denise-Link FarajAli, then guide a discussion in ways that show how the theme of a poem can connect to students' lives.

B. Following the pre-reading activities, we suggest a silent reading period in which learners go through the story at their own pace for general meaning. This can be followed by an opportunity to retell the story to partners, discuss the text in depth, or find out which of the learners' questions were found in the story. The questions at the bottom of the page are intended to start a group discussion that will help learners focus on the unit theme by relating the opening story to their own experiences as immigrants and as language learners. For the second reading, we suggest that you read the story aloud (or play the tape) at normal speed, then invite learners to express their reactions to the story or ask about details or vocabulary items that remain unclear.

2 In "Playing with Story Language," learners are given a closer look at language forms and conventions used to construct written texts. In Parts A and B, learners concentrate on listening for, then converting personal pronouns, while Part C directs learners' attention to the words and phrases used to establish reference in consecutive sentences. Following these activities, you may want to ask students to summarize these forms, and to suggest ways they can use them in their own writing.

FIELD TESTERS' NOTES • • •

1 *To prepare for reading, I try to focus in on the vocabulary the students will encounter. To do so, I initiate a discussion on some aspect of the listening text, drawing on the students' own experiences and listing on the board, the vocabulary they use or seem to be reaching for. If a relevant picture exists, I always use it because I have found that even the most reserved student can say a little something about a picture.*

Denise L. Link-FarajAli
Prince Georges County Refugee Training Program
Bladensburg, MD

A. *In order to prepare students for Unit 1, I first needed to introduce the concept of poetry. To do so, I used the "old standby" by Robert Frost about a road diverging in the woods and the decision to take the road less traveled, "which made all the difference." I tried to elicit various decisions students had made in their lives— both positive and negative—likening, in the end, Frost's divergence to their own specific decisions to leave their countries and come to America. This truly struck a chord with the students!*

Denise L. Link-FarajAli
Prince Georges County Refugee Training Program
Bladensburg, MD

B. *I read the story aloud to the class, talked about some of the vocabulary, then they read it again. Although it was a bit long, most of the students understood and enjoyed it.*

Mary K. Shea
ESL Adult Education Teacher
Annandale, VA

③ Doing It in English: Describing Yourself

A. Do you remember the words Mariano Ramos Hernandez used to describe himself?

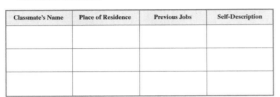

> "I've been a hospital worker, a bus boy, a waiter, and a cook. I call myself a lucky guy. I've always lived the way you see me now—poor and humble, but happy."

B. Get to know three of your classmates. Find out their names and where they live. Ask what kind of jobs they have had. Then ask what words they use to describe themselves. Take notes in the chart below.

Classmate's Name	Place of Residence	Previous Jobs	Self-Description

C. Introduce one of the classmates you interviewed to the rest of the class. Use the notes from your chart.

In this photo, Cesar is walking in the Puerto Rican parade in New Haven.

> "This is Cesar Ramirez. He lives in New Haven, Connecticut. He's been a taxi driver and a salesman. He's healthy, happy, and strong."

Subject Complements

After any form of the verb *be*, use a noun, a noun phrase, or an adjective.

He's always been a poet.
I'm not rich, but I'm healthy and strong.

④ Sharing Experiences: Describing Other People

A. Read these two examples of how Mariano described other people in his story.

"I wrote another one for my best friend, a girl *who went to school with me*."

"I like my poetry to be understood, even by people *who have no education at all*."

B. Work with a partner. Look at the photograph. How can Ramon Vasquez identify himself in the Puerto Rican parade? Complete his description.

Relative Clauses with *Who*

A **relative clause** tells more about the noun it follows. When a relative clause begins with *who*, it gives more information about a person.

Mariano Ramos Hernandez is a poet who writes in both Spanish and English.

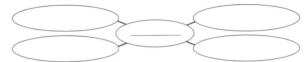
I'm the guy who

C. Think of a person you know very well. Write the person's name in the center of the web diagram below.

D. Complete this sentence about the person you are thinking of in as many different ways as you can.

_____ is a person who _____

Write your sentence completions in the circles around the person's name on the web diagram.

E. Describe the person to a partner. Explain his or her relationship to you, then make sentences based on your web diagram.

INSTRUCTOR'S JOURNAL

Page 4
Workbook: pages 2–3

Correlates with:

Page 5
Workbook: page 4
Activity Master: page 1

4 • • •

AUTHORS' NOTES • • •

3   This page offers an opportunity for learners to get to know each other while informally reviewing the use of nouns, noun phrases, and adjectives as subject complements. As in all levels of *Collaborations*, our approach is to provide learners with a sample of natural language used in the story, then invite them to interact in meaningful ways by asking for information from classmates, sharing their own experiences and perspectives, or expressing their reactions to new language events. The basic structure modeled in Part A is summarized in the box in the lower right corner of the page. Learners who need review or clarification of the terms used in the summary boxes can refer to the Glossary of Grammatical Terms on pages 103–104. We have also included a list of Irregular Verbs (page 105).

4   **B.** The photograph on this page, taken at the Puerto Rican Parade in New Haven, invites students to be creative in completing the man's description of himself in a crowd. Invite partners to read their sentences aloud. As a follow-up, you could also ask learners to imagine a group photograph of the whole class, then identify themselves in the picture using relative clauses.

   C.–D. In this two step process, learners practice the learning strategy of recalling and organizing information on their own, then communicating it in a specific way to a partner. If students are not familiar with using graphic organizers, we recommend drawing an empty web diagram on the board or on a blank transparency, then talk the class through the activity, using "think aloud" natural language that reflects your decision-making process. For example,

   Let's see, hmmm . . . someone I know very well. OK, I guess my sister is someone I really do know very well. What can I say about her? Wait a minute, first I'll write her name in the center circle (pause) Marianne, her last name too? Yes, all right, it's Lorenzelli. Now what can I tell my partner about Marianne? She doesn't know her at all. Well, to begin with, Marianne is a person who gets along with just about everybody. She's a real "people" person . . . and so on.

FIELD TESTERS' NOTES • • •

3   *The most positive reactions from students were always prompted by the small group or pair activities. I'm very fortunate to have a multi-cultural group where, upon pairing, studetns are forced to speak to each other, using the target language to complete a given task.*

   I found that new friendships were born in this very way, and here, especially in the "Self-Description" on page 4.

                              Denise L. Link-FarajAli
Prince Georges County Refugee Training Program
                              Bladensburg, MD

4   *C.–D. The web diagram and attendant activities served as a unifying activity for our class. My class decided to use the names of two teachers, whom they were eager to describe. Once someone volunteered the names, they talked eagerly. They stayed on task, laughing and writing. It was amazing to see how accurate a description of us they had rendered in a short time.*

                              Denise L. Link-FarajAli
Prince Georges County Refugee Training Program
                              Bladensburg, MD

   The web diagram was a new idea for most of my students. After trying it out, they understood its value and liked it.

                              Mary K. Shea
                    ESL Adult Education Teacher
                              Annandale, VA

A. Read part of Mariano Ramos Hernandez' poem "Dos Patrias" (Two Lands) in Spanish or in English.

> **Dos Patrias**
>
> *Soy un hombre*
> *y con dos patrias*
> *con dos nombres*
> *dos historias*
> *dos banderas*
> *dos culturas diferentes*
> *dos lenguajes*
> *son dos patrias*
> *dos amores*

> **Two Lands**
>
> *I am a man*
> *with two lands*
> *with two names*
> *two histories*
> *two flags*
> *two different cultures*
> *two languages*
> *of two lands*
> *two loves*

(from *Intimate Verses* by Mariano Ramos Hernandez, permission granted by the author)

B. Discuss your reaction to "Two Lands" with a partner. Use these questions as a guide.

- Do you like the poem?
- What do you like or dislike about it?
- What do you think "two loves" in the last line means?
- How does it make you feel?

C. Get together with another set of partners who have discussed the same lines. Compare your reactions.

D. Think of a few lines of a poem or song in your native language. Share them with your group, both in your native language and in English. Invite your classmates to discuss their reactions.

 Learning About
Each Other: Personal Accomplishments and Talents

A. Read about Mariano Ramos Hernandez' first book of poems.

> I published this collection of poetry, "Desde la Distancia," (From a Distance) in 1991. Of course, I'm very proud of it. The title means that my life is here, but my worries and my mind are in Puerto Rico. I call it that, because from a distance, it was my anguish. These are the poems I've written since I was a little boy. Some of them are the stories my mother taught me. All of the poems in this book are in Spanish, but I do write poems in English sometimes.

B. Discuss these questions with a partner.

- What special ability does Mariano Ramos have?
- How has he used this ability?

C. A *talent* is a special ability to do something, such as write poetry, dance, or play music. An *accomplishment* is anything you have done that you are proud of. What are your talents? What have you accomplished in your life so far? Tell a partner. Take notes in the chart.

	Me	My Partner
Talents		
Accomplishments		

D. Tell the class about your partner's accomplishments and talents.

INSTRUCTOR'S JOURNAL

AUTHORS' NOTES . . .

5 A. We have found that many language learners respond to poetry as a catalyst for tapping a common experience and engaging them in less restrictive forms of communication that "touch the soul" as well as challenge the intellect. "Dos Patrias" is presented in both Spanish and English here to illustrate the poet's reflection on bilingual and bicultural existence. However, learners who are not Spanish speakers should easily be able to relate to the experience; you may even want to ask the class to translate the poem into various languages and make a bulletin board display of the results.

B.–C. We have orchestrated this activity as a think-pair-share activity in order for learners to experience a slowly expanding circle of conversation as they express their personal reactions to the poem. We hope that through this and other techniques used throughout the book, students will gain experience in classroom discussion skills that will eventually enable them to participate in academic settings with confidence and ease.

6 A. The walls in Mariano Ramos Hernandez' home office are covered with diplomas, awards, and photographs documenting his life's accomplishments. As he spoke of his poetry, his face never failed to light up with pride. Before students read the paragraph describing "Desde La Distancia," you could remind them that the poet had not had an easy life, or the benefits of a high-level education. You may also want to introduce the term "self-made person" and ask if they know of any others.

D. Telling the class about a partner's talents and abilities, rather than their own, relieves students of having to "brag" about themselves, a tendency that is not considered admirable in many of the world's cultures. On the other hand, it gives them experience in relating personal traits and achievements in a relatively formal setting.

FIELD TESTERS' NOTES . . .

5 *This was a real challenge for my students, but I believe they liked doing it.*

Mary K. Shea
ESL Adult Education Teacher
Annandale, VA

B.–C. *The poem "Dos Patrios" proved another very unifying experience for the class. A discussion ensued as to the meaning. Students wanted to dwell at length on what each line meant and offer different interpretations .*
Fascinating . . . and all in English!

Denise L. Link-FarajAli
Prince Georges County Refugee Program
Bladensburg, MD

6 A. *Colombian nun who has been here for nine years was excited about this word, "accomplishments." She works with the Spanish community as a counselor and religious educator, and had never heard or understood the word before. She said it stayed in her mind all day, and she kept thinking about it.*

Mary K. Shea
ESL Adult Education Teacher
Annandale, VA

D. *Discussing one's talents proved very timely to my group as we were about to embark on "Job Club," where the students need to learn to sell themselves in an interview situation. Bravo on a deft transition to this seemingly unique American assertiveness.*

Denise L. Link-FarajAli
Prince Georges County Refugee Training Program
Bladensburg, MD

Learning About
                  Each Other: Things We're Proud Of

 A. Discuss the event in this photograph with a partner. Why do you think the people in this community are celebrating? What are they proud of?

 **B.** Explain something you are proud of or happy about to a small group of your classmates.

Using Preposition Clusters

An adjective is often used with a preposition following a form of the verb *be.* Together, the adjective + preposition are called a **preposition cluster.** After a preposition cluster such as *proud of, happy about, sure of,* you can use (a) a noun, (b) a gerund phrase, or (c) a noun clause beginning with *what* or *who.*

Mariano is **proud of** { his poetry / working hard / who he is }

I'm happy about my new job. What about you?

I'm proud of being Puerto Rican.

Puerto Rico is an island in the Caribbean Sea, east of Haiti and the Dominican Republic. The population of Puerto Rico is 3,522,520, and the capital is San Juan. Puerto Rico was a colony of Spain until 1898, when it became a possession of the United States as a result of the Spanish-American War. Puerto Ricans were granted U.S. citizenship in 1917, and the Commonwealth of Puerto Rico was established in 1952. Since the turn of the century, over 2.5 million Puerto Ricans have migrated to Hawaii, New York City, and the New England states to work at various jobs in agriculture and industry.

 Sharing
              Experiences: Cultural Traditions in North America

A. Discuss ways the people in these photographs are maintaining traditions from their native lands.

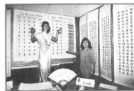

B. How do you maintain cultural traditions in North America? Share your experiences and ideas.

C. Do you think it is important to maintain traditions from your native land in North America? Check (✔) the statement that you agree with most. Explain your opinion to your group.

It's not very important to me. ❑

It's somewhat important to me. ❑

It's very important to me. ❑

INSTRUCTOR'S JOURNAL

AUTHORS' NOTES ● ● ●

7   The photographs on pages 8 and 9 are intended to spark conversation about the many ways immigrants maintain their home cultural traditions. Discussion topics can alternate between specific and general questions about how the people in the photographs and the learners themselves describe and celebrate the aspects of their lives they are proud of. You may want to scan the pages ahead to choose (or ask the class to choose) activities that are most appropriate for your group.

   A. The group of Puerto Rican musicians in this photograph are celebrating Christmas, as many students will recognize from the decorated tree in the background.

   B. The relatively complex concept of preposition clusters and their use can be further illustrated by having the class generate a list of additional clusters and make sentences using them. For further practice with preposition clusters, see page 9 in the *Workbook*.

   The geographical information at the bottom of the page is presented in response to our reviewers and field testers, who report their students' intense interest in learning more about each others' homelands. Students who wish to acquire or practice library research skills are given the opportunity to do so in the "Options for Learning," near the end of each unit.

8   This small-group discussion page gives learners further opportunities to share their knowledge and ideas informally while preparing for the more academic activities on pages 10, 11, and 12.

   For a related discussion of cultural differences in interpersonal communication, see *Activity Masters*, page 4. This activity has proven particularly successful with ethnically diverse groups.

FIELD TESTERS' NOTES ● ● ●

7   *Talking about pictures has always been a favorite device of mine to get otherwise reticent students to open up, and here are pictures galore of various cultures throughout the unit.*

Denise L. Link-FarajAli
Prince Georges County Refugee Training Program
Bladensburg, MD

8   *I used activities 7, 8, and 9 in my upper intermediate/advanced class. We had great pair, small group, and whole group discussions—in fact, it lasted $2\frac{1}{2}$ hours!*

Mary Leonard
Wyoming Community Education
Wyoming, MI

9 **Think It Over:** Is America a Melting Pot?

 A. Look at the cartoon. What do you think it means? Talk it over with a partner. Then read the explanation of the term, "Melting Pot" in the box below.

> "The Melting Pot" is the name of a play about immigrants written by Israel Zangwill. In the play, which opened in Washington, D.C. in 1908, one of the characters declared:
>
> "America is . . . the great Melting Pot where all the races of Europe are melting and reforming . . . Germans and Frenchmen, Irishmen and Englishmen, Jews and Russians—into the Crucible with you all! God is making the American!"
>
> Although very few Americans living today have seen Zangwill's play, the term "melting pot" is still widely used and discussed. Basically, it is a metaphor* for becoming a new person in a new land. People who support the melting pot idea believe that newcomers should "become American" as quickly as possible. That is, they should speak only English, wear baseball caps, and eat apple pie.

Reading Strategy

Cartoons, drawings, and photographs are different types of illustrations. Illustrations help readers understand the meaning of new ideas.

*metaphor—a word or phrase used to stand for something different than its usual meaning. A metaphor is one type of figure of speech.

 B. Reread the last sentence in the box. Have you "become American" in these ways? With your partner, brainstorm some of the other ways newcomers change when they come to America.

Learning Strategy

Listen and read for the ways metaphors are used in English. Ask teachers or friends to help you clarify the meanings of these terms.

C. Here are two other metaphors people sometimes use to represent ways people of different cultures and languages live together in North America. Work with your partner to invent a third metaphor of your own. Share it with the class.

Melting Pot,
Salad Bowl,
Patchwork Quilt,

---

 10 **Doing It in English:** Expressing and Recording Opinions

A. Should languages other than English be used in your ESL classroom? Check (✔) your opinion:

1. English only ☐
2. English most of the time ☐
3. Not sure ☐

B. Discuss your opinion with a small group of classmates. If you checked "English most of the time," explain exactly when using other languages might be helpful. If you checked "Not sure," explain what questions or doubts you have.

C. Count the different opinions in your group and report to the class. Then complete the report below for the whole class.

OPINION SURVEY

Number of students who . . .

1. support "English only" _____
2. support "English plus*" _____
3. are not sure _____

*English and one or more other languages

D. The graph below shows the results of a similar opinion survey in a large North American city that has a large French-speaking population. Use the information in the graph to complete the sentences below.

Should the street signs in our city be in both English and French?

1. The majority of people surveyed felt that _____.
2. _____ of those asked said that the new signs should be in both English and French.
3. _____ had not made up their minds.

INSTRUCTOR'S JOURNAL

Page 10	Correlates with:	Page 11
Transparency: page 12		Workbook: page 11
Workbook: page 10		

10 • • •

AUTHORS' NOTES . . .

9 **A.** Although virtually all languages include metaphors, the ways they are used in English may be new and sometimes confusing to your students. The specific concept of the Melting Pot and the story of how the term originated are intended to give students a taste of history as well as to introduce them to strategies for understanding the meanings of new terms. You could start by discussing the cartoon. Explain the character of Uncle Sam and ask students to guess what is going on in the pot. Then read the passage silently and return to the cartoon to see if their explanations have changed.

After discussing the general meaning of the passage, it is helpful to focus upon specific vocabulary items. In general, we have found that inviting students to use context and visual clues to guess meaning before confirming with definitions, explanations, or synonyms helps learners build independent reading strategies over the long term.

C. The alternative metaphors and the invitation to students to create their own demonstrate the individuality of expression that is possible with language. For fun, you might want to ask students to illustrate their original metaphors on the board or on a blank transparency for group display.

10 **A.–C.** This sequence challenges learners to think, discuss individual opinions, then survey the attitudes of their classmates. As with other skill-building activities, we recommend pausing after the last step to ask learners to reflect briefly on the process they have just completed and suggest ways they might be able to apply what they are learning to their lives outside the ESL classroom.

D. This is the first of many graph exercises included at this level to help learners strengthen and diversify their academic reading skills. Possible compilations include:

1. The majority of people surveyed felt that *street signs should only be in one language.*
2. *Fifty four percent (54%)* of those asked said that new street signs should be in both English and French.
3. *Thirteen percent (13%) of those asked* had not made up their minds.

FIELD TESTERS' NOTES . . .

9 **A.** *My students and I both enjoyed learning about the origins of the Melting Pot metaphor and comparing it to the Salad Bowl and Patchwork Quilt analogies of America. Time permitting, I would bring in an actual "patchwork quilt" from home, explaining how each unique patch together creates a unified whole. From there, I would introduce the class to our nearby Amish culture—a people who happen to make beautiful quilts—as a classic example of how a culture remains true to itself within America. Again, if time permitted, I would conclude with a showing of the video, "Witness."*
Denise L. Link-FarajAli
Prince Georges County Refugee Training Program
Bladensburg, MD

10 *The class survey on page 11 was a lot of fun. Everyone voted! I used "voting sticks" with "yes" and "no" printed on opposite sides; students feel more safe and secure in raising their sticks as opposed to raising their hands.*

Denise L. Link-FarajAli
Prince Georges County Refugee Training Program
Bladensburg, MD

E. Work with a partner. Based on the results of your class survey, draw lines and label the sections of the graph below. Then write three sentences that describe your graph.

F. How do you feel about the role of English in your life outside the classroom? Read over the list below. Which of these things should people living in North America be able to do only in English? Which things should they be able to do in their first languages or in English?

	English Only	English Plus (English or Native Language)
Open a bank account.	❑	❑
Get a job.	❑	❑
Take a driver's license exam.	❑	❑
Participate in religious services.	❑	❑
Get medical help.	❑	❑
Get information about government programs.	❑	❑
Become a citizen of the U.S. or Canada.	❑	❑
(other) _____	❑	❑
	❑	❑

G. Tell your group which items on the list you checked and explain why.

Journal Writing: People and Ideas

In your journal, describe yourself or someone you know very well. These are some things you might want to include:

- where you come from
- some things you have done
- where you live and work now
- some things you are proud of

Write more about *your* experience in this country. Explain why you are learning English, and what your goals are. Give examples of where it is important to use English, and in what situations you prefer to communicate in your native language.

Other Voices from North America

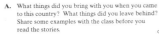
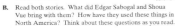

A. What things did you bring with you when you came to this country? What things did you leave behind? Share some examples with the class before you read the stories.

B. Read both stories. What did Edgar Sabogal and Shoua Vue bring with them? How have they used these things in North America? Think about these questions as you read.

C. Circle the words you want to remember.

I see a lot of emptiness in North American cities. In New England, the cities are colder, and the colors are dull and gray. People are isolated from each other. They are crowded together into small spaces, but they don't communicate.

When I look at a city, I have this kind of reaction. Something inside of me is warm, maybe because I am from a place that is close to the Equator, where the sun is directly overhead. As a child, I was used to seeing green any time of day. So now, when I paint a city here in New England, I add the colors.

Sometimes when North Americans look at my paintings, they are shocked because I have a different way of looking at cities. Bright colors like purple, green, and orange are too confusing for some people. I just want people to see my work. I want to say to them, "These are my colors!"

Edgar Sabogal is a fine artist who works in Holyoke, Massachusetts. He is originally from Colombia.

We left Laos with all those seeds and plants that are good for healing. We carried them in the boat crossing the Mekong River and planted them again when we got to the camp in Thailand. Three years later we took them with us to America. They are precious to us. Our forefathers had brought them when they moved from China to Laos over a hundred years ago. Here in San Diego some of the plants grow better than others, but between my mother and me, we haven't lost any yet.

I also use Tylenol® and Anacin®, and sometimes Contac®, but not often. Our medicine is different. It makes the body strong. We use it inside and outside. I grow about ten different kinds. Some taste very good, and I put them into chicken soup.

Shoua Vue is a member of the Hmong minority group from Laos. She lives with her family in San Diego, California.

INSTRUCTOR'S JOURNAL

AUTHORS' NOTES • • •

10 E. This step in the pie graph sequence asks students to construct their own graph based on the results of the class language use survey. You might want to invite students to draw their graphs on the board or on a transparency for group display. Note that the "slices" of the pie can appear in any position, and can be distinguished in various ways (for example using colors, shading, or patterns).

11 We have found that students who have trouble expressing themselves orally often keep great journals. In this journal-writing activity, as in those found elsewhere in the book, students are given the opportunity to explore their ideas, relate their personal experiences, and react to the stories in writing. It is important to emphasize that this is a place for students to have a private written conversation with their teacher in which real thoughts and ideas are exchanged using personal, informal language. Advise students that the questions are to be used as a guide, but they should feel free to express other things on their minds as well.

In your half of the "conversation," we believe it is important to focus on content rather than on aspects of grammar or mechanics and to use a personal, encouraging tone in responding to students' ideas.

We recommend that journals be kept confidential, and that a student-writer be consulted before anything from his or her journal is shared with the class.

12 The "Other Voices from North America" stories, near the end of each unit, express themes and describe experiences to which adult learners can easily relate, making it easier to grasp the general message despite the presence of new vocabulary. As a source of reading pleasure as well as useful information, these stories offer students the opportunity to enrich their vocabulary as they become more experienced readers. In a multi-level class, you might well want to let students choose between these stories and the editorial on the following page.

FIELD TESTERS' NOTES • • •

13 Doing It in English: Reading Newspaper Editorials

A. In an *editorial*, the writer expresses an opinion about a certain topic. The editorial below appeared in a newspaper in Hartford, the capital of Connecticut. Read the editorial, then decide whether you agree or disagree with the writer's main point.

> **Reading Strategy**
>
> As you read, look for the main point. Consider the examples and reasons the writer uses to support his or her opinion.

A Lesson from My American Grandmother
by John Andrews

My elderly grandmother, who arrived in this country from Scotland in 1922, was recently in an automobile accident. At the hospital, the doctors who were treating her could not understand a word of the strange language she was speaking. They thought she had gone crazy. Just then, a nurse who had recently immigrated from Scotland arrived at her bedside, stopped for a moment to listen to the familiar sounds. The nurse reported to the doctors that there was nothing at all wrong with the old lady's brain. She was not off her rocker. She had simply gone back to Gaelic, the language of her early childhood.

I can't help but think sometimes that the supporters of the English-as-a-national-language movement are just as shortsighted as the doctors who treated my grandmother. As the children and grandchildren of immigrants ourselves, we must never forget that languages other than English are part of our heritage, too. Speaking another language should not make anyone strange, different, or less American.

> **IDIOMS**
> off her rocker
> the American dream
> wall of fear

As a matter of fact, what we love best about America—the promise of freedom and the chance for a better life—are the very same values our most recent immigrants cherish. The Iranian grocer, the Somali taxi driver, the Bosnian refugee all share this hope. Many of these newcomers have been through much more hardship than any of us can even imagine. The fact that they may not yet speak perfect English has nothing to do with their loyalty to their new homeland, or to their willingness to work hard to achieve the American dream.

The desire of our new immigrants to keep cultural traditions alive does not conflict with their desire to become Americans. According to the principle of religious freedom, upon which this country was founded, there is no reason why a Cambodian temple, a Russian church, or a Moroccan mosque, should not be warmly welcomed here. Likewise, when we think of freedom of speech, we must not insist that immigrants abandon their native languages as they learn English. We must instead get rid of the wall of fear that arises from the fact that many of us do not speak other languages. We must learn to celebrate differences as we learn more about each other. As my grandmother would say, we will be richer for it.

B. Check the sentence that best expresses the writer's main point.

❑ The doctors had never heard my grandmother's native language before.

❑ Immigrants should try harder to be like other Americans.

❑ New Americans should feel free to maintain their languages and cultural traditions.

 C. Do you agree or disagree with the writer's main point? Explain your reasons to a partner.

 14 Bringing the Outside In: Conducting a Community Survey

Take your own survey of opinions in your local community. Ask several of your teachers, friends, or family members about the importance of maintaining cultural traditions in North America.

With the class, decide on the questions you want to ask. Work with a partner to conduct short interviews. Bring the results to class. With the help of your teacher, you may present the results in the form of a chart.

These are the questions one class wrote:

> *How do you maintain cultural traditions in North America?*
> *Where do you communicate mainly in English?*
> *Where do you communicate mainly in your native language?*
> *Do you agree with "English only" or "English plus?"*

 15 Ideas for Action: Planning a Cultural Event

A. Plan a cultural event in which you and your classmates demonstrate ways of maintaining cultural traditions. Your plan need not be complicated or expensive. Work with a small group to work out the details. Include these steps in your planning.

1. Decide on a time and date.
2. Decide who you want to invite.
3. Plan how you will advertise the event.
4. Put together a program. Decide what each person in your group will do. (examples: read a poem, share some food, demonstrate a custom)
5. Estimate how much the event will cost and suggest ways of paying for it.

B. Present your group's plan to the whole class. When all the plans have been presented, vote on the best plan for your situation.

C. With your teacher's help, decide as a class if you actually want to carry out the plan. If everyone agrees it is a good idea, decide what the next steps should be.

INSTRUCTOR'S JOURNAL

AUTHORS' NOTES • • •

13 The newspaper editorial on this page offers a more challenging task to students who wish to sharpen their skills and broaden their reading experience. If possible, bring a newspaper to class and show students the editorial page. Explain that the purpose of an editorial is to express the writer's (or the newspaper's) opinion. Ask students how this differs from the purpose of news stories. To preview "A Lesson from My American Grandmother," ask students to speculate on what the title might mean. You might also want to write these questions on the board:

> *What is the topic?*
> *What is the writer's opinion about the topic?*
> *What is your opinion?*

As with other readings at this level, we recommend an initial silent reading period in which students read the whole passage and perform the two activities (Parts B–C) before returning to the text to clarify unfamiliar terms, discuss details, or analyze language use. Although students may initially be reluctant to approach a new text in this way, they will realize its advantages as they gain confidence and build strategies as mature, independent readers.

14 "Bringing the Outside In," which occurs near the end of each unit, motivates students to interact with each other on the basis of resources from the world outside the classroom. In this unit, students are instructed to take their own survey of opinions in their local communities. In our experience, learners have been more successful at carrying out these types of community research activities when they work in pairs and ask questions of people they already know. If getting around to conduct interviews is a problem, encourage learners to use the telephone to communicate with their "respondents." Remind learners that it is important to take good notes (or tape record their interviews) in order to get the necessary information.

15 The purpose of "Ideas For Action" is to focus learners' attention on how they can use the language and literacy skills they have learned to transform some aspect of their lives, in this case how they can plan a cultural event for presentation to a wider audience. During this activity, it is not unusual for learners to become so intensely involved in the planning that they may forget time constraints. If your group decides to actually carry out the plan, it may be necessary to stipulate that subsequent preparations and planning sessions take place outside regular class hours.

FIELDTESTERS' NOTES • • •

15 *Another very coalescing activity for our class was the cultural event we planned for the following week: an informal potluck, featuring foods from the students' home countries.*

Denise L. Link-FarajAli
Prince Georges County Refugee Training Program
Bladensburg, MD

16 Options for Learning: Communicating About Cultural Traditions

A. What do you want to tell people about yourself or your culture?
Check (✔) your answers. Add other ideas if you wish.

	Already Do	Want to Learn	Not Interested
Locate information about your country or culture.			
Explain a cultural tradition or custom.			
Write a letter to a newspaper expressing your opinion.			
Form an organization for maintaining your language and culture.			
Other? _____			

17 Looking Back

Think about your learning. Complete this form. Then tell the class your ideas.

A. The most useful thing I learned in this unit was _____

_____ .

B. I would still like to learn _____ .

C. I learned the most by working

_____ alone.   _____ with a partner.   _____ with a group.

D. The activity I liked best was 1 2 3 4 5 6 7 8 9 10 11 12 13 14 15 16

because _____ .

E. The activity I liked least was 1 2 3 4 5 6 7 8 9 10 11 12 13 14 15 16

because _____ .

18 Learning Log

Checklist for Learning

I. **Vocabulary:** Add more words and phrases to each list. Check (✔) the ones you want to remember. For extra practice, write sentences with the new words and phrases.

Words to Describe People
_____ lucky
_____ humble
_____ _____
_____ _____
_____ _____
_____ _____

IDIOMS
_____ a lucky guy
_____ _____
_____ _____
_____ _____

Occupations
_____ waiter
_____ busboy
_____ _____
_____ _____
_____ _____
_____ _____

Personal Talents
_____ sing
_____ dance
_____ _____
_____ _____
_____ _____
_____ _____

Ways of Maintaining Cultural Traditions
_____ speaking native languages
_____ writing poetry
_____ _____
_____ _____
_____ _____
_____ _____

II. **Language:** Check (✔) what you can do in English. Add more ideas if you wish.

I can
_____ describe myself or a person I know well
_____ recognize words that stand for times, places, and things in a reading passage
_____ explain something you are proud of or happy about
_____ read and discuss a poem
_____ talk about your personal talents and accomplishments
_____ recognize and interpret metaphors
_____ ask for, express, and discuss personal opinions
_____ _____
_____ _____

III. **Listening:** Listen to the Review Interview at the end of Unit 1. Ask your teacher for the *Collaborations* worksheet.

INSTRUCTOR'S JOURNAL

Page 16	Correlates with:	Page 17
Activity Masters: pages 7–10		**Activity Master: page 11**
Workbook: page 13		**Audiotape: Review Interview**
		Workbook: page 14

AUTHORS' NOTES • • •

16 The "Options for Learning" activity provides learners the opportunity to work on developing specific competencies relevant to their situations and needs. Each of the skills on the list is correlated to a Unit 1 *Activity Master,* (pp. 7–10), which can be copied and distributed as needed. We suggest that you first ask all of your students to fill out the form and report to a partner (Part B). Then, based on their "Want to Learn" choices, distribute the relevant worksheets. Students may work as individuals, with partners, or in small groups as you circulate and act as a resource person. To wrap up the work session, you might want to ask students to reflect on what they learned and its value to them in terms of their language learning goals.

17 As in the previous books in this series, we have included an invitation to "Look Back" in each unit, to foster reflection on what has been learned as well as to ask learners to comment on what did and did not work for them. Adults often reflect critically on their educational experiences (sometimes by voting with their feet!). This activity gives them an opportunity to voice these reflections where it matters—to their teachers and to one another. In the *Workbook,* "Test Yourself" and "Learning Diary" provide additional tools for self-assessment.

   Although learners are not likely to fully realize their language goals in the course of one term or semester, periodic and regular reflection will enable them to look back on how far they have come. As they articulate what they know, what they want to learn more about, and what they liked and disliked, you will also gain important insights into both their goals and preferred learning styles. An added bonus is that as students listen to each other, they will become more aware of the diversity of learning styles among their classmates and will hopefully develop a greater appreciation of some of the activities they had previously thought were of limited value.

18 The "Checklist for Learning" at the end of every unit offers learners the opportunity to monitor, in a very concrete and specific way, language skills they have learned. It also provides a way to look back over time, to see how much has been retained. Stress that the checklist is for individual self-assessment. However, when students have finished checking off Parts I and II of the list, you might want to invite requests for specific review within the unit before moving on.

   Part III of the Checklist, the Review Interview, can be carried out as a group listening activity. Students will need copies of *Activity Master 11*. Play the final section of the Unit 1 Audiotape (Review Interview) and let students complete the listening task on their own.

FIELD TESTERS' NOTES • • •

17 *This was a good opportunity to review the unit. We went back through the week to see what we had accomplished.*

Mary K. Shea
ESL Adult Education Teacher
Annandale, VA

Unit 2

Sharing Strategies in Harrisburg, Pennsylvania

The first stories in this chapter come from Harrisburg, the capital of Pennsylvania. Pennsylvania was founded in 1681 by William Penn on land given to him by King Charles II of England in payment of a debt. In part because of Penn's religious beliefs, the colony quickly became a haven for religious dissenters and other immigrants. Immigrants have come to Pennsylvania from many parts of Europe through the 300 years of its history. Now people emigrate to Harrisburg from Russia, Vietnam, Iraq, Ethiopia, and many other places. They learn English and North American culture, and they learn to study together at programs such as those run by the Immigration and Refugee Services of Catholic Charities of Harrisburg.

Pennsylvania

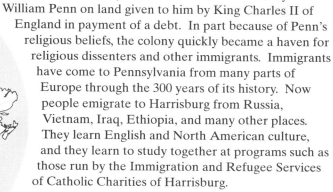

Four Stories from Harrisburg

A. What are some effective ways to learn English? How can people learn and teach at the same time? Are your goals similar to others' in your class? Compare your ideas.

B. As you read the stories, compare the philosophies and goals of these people with those of your classmates, instructors, and yourself.

Ali shares his ideas in one of Michael's classes at Immigration and Refugee Services of Catholic Charities.

Iraq contains the fertile valleys of the Tigris and Euphrates rivers where Mesopotamia once flourished. About 97 percent of Iraq's 21 million people are Muslims. Under the rule of Saddam Hussein, the war with Iran and the 1991 Gulf War have caused terrible damage to the people and the country of Iraq.

Ali Al-Shermery's Story

I am from Basra, Iraq. I came here six months ago. I have a job, and I always come to school. I am a carpet installer. I was an Arabic teacher in Iraq. In 1991, I was part of the uprising against Saddam Hussein. Later, I couldn't live in my country, and I moved to Saudi Arabia. I came here in 1994. Two days a week I study English. Speaking is easiest for me. I'm not good, but, you know, I'm trying. So, sometimes I can't read, sometimes I can't write, but I can speak. I don't need a translator. If I don't speak English, I won't eat. I've only studied English here. I listen to music, I watch T.V., and I listen to different people. I listen to different dialects. I have to understand. After five years, if Saddam Hussein dies, I will go back to my home again. I think I want to be a teacher for kids, or maybe, I will be a businessman.

Michael studied many languages. Now he wants to help his community.

Michael Westover's Story

I was born in Augusta, Georgia. I've lived in Harrisburg since 1981, and I've been a teacher with Catholic Charities since 1991. I have one class in the morning that prepares people to work, and the main thing I want them to be able to do at work is to speak to co-workers and their bosses. I think if they can do that, they can learn everything else on the job. I think the main thrust in my night class is to make people from different cultures work together peaceably. We talk about the differences in religions. In the evening, I have Catholics, Muslims, and Jews all together. I make them talk about the similarities and the differences and help them to respect their differences and enjoy their similarities. I do the same thing with education and social status. I show them that they are in the same boat when it comes to English and that they have to help each other and that really wakes them up.

IDIOMS
main thrust
in the same boat
wakes them up

Izrail Dubrovitsky's Story

I was an electrical engineer in Russia. I had that job for 47 years. Now I have no job; I am a pensioner. The people in the United States are very friendly to people who come from other countries. I study here for two hours, four days a week. In my country, I had learned German. Before I came to the United States, I studied English for just two months. Because I come from another country, I have many problems, and I need many documents. The official papers come to my mailbox, and I have to answer them. At first, when I came to the United States, I needed to look at every word in my dictionary. I translated the sentences with my dictionary. I needed to translate many times because I couldn't understand which definitions were proper for me. At home, I watch T.V., but I don't understand the way people are talking. I want to have more conversations with native speakers.

Izrail and Faina, who are married, study together at school. At home they speak Russian to each other.

Learning Strategy
In a good dictionary you can find definitions, grammar, idioms, pronunciation, and the history of words.

Faina Belkina's Story

For 40 years I was a neurologist in Russia. Now, life is difficult for me. I read books. I read better now, but I don't understand conversation well. I also watch TV. The conversation on TV is very fast, and sometimes I don't understand the situation. In class, we do reading one day, grammar another day, and we also use the dictionary. Studying in the class is very good. My progress in reading and writing is better than in conversation.

I live in a very big building with many neighbors. With a very nice neighbor, we celebrate many American holidays. At home, I do homework, I read, and I watch TV.

Russia is the largest country in the world. It covers 11 of the world's time zones. Between 1922 and 1991, Russia was the most powerful republic of the Soviet Union. Now, Russia is in a period of political, social, and economic change.

INSTRUCTOR'S JOURNAL

Page 20	Correlates with:	Page 21
Audiotape		Audiotape
Transparencies: page 5		Transparencies: page 5
Workbook: pages 16, 21		Workbook: pages 16, 21

AUTHORS' NOTES • • •

1 **A.** Identifying strategies and goals are the underlying tasks of this unit, so, right from the beginning, we want learners to reflect on the ways and the reasons they learn. The synergy between learning and teaching can be so powerful that we want learners to reflect on that, also. You and your class can work on the questions the way you choose: brainstorming a list in the whole group, writing to be shared and compared in the days to come, or through partner interviews.

We hope that learners will begin to scrutinize their own educational assumptions, so that they can be successful not only in learning English, but also as they continue their education here in North America.

B. We suggest you use page 5 of the *Transparencies* for pre-reading because Ali Al-Shermery's energy is contagious in this larger photo. In some ways, the photos of Ali and of Izrail and Faina depict two ways of learning, one "modern" and one more "traditional." We think that the class conversation that may arise here, can continue throughout this unit.

The four stories provide the beginning of a "patchwork quilt" of learners and teachers that will grow as your students compare experiences and strategies. Initially, in a group of four, learners could read just one story and retell it to the others in their own group or another group. Then play the audiotape as the class reads along. Next, review the questions as a whole group, encouraging the learners to look at both similarities and differences when they make comparisons.

Throughout the text, you will find opportunities for detours. Here, you could work in groups to investigate dictionaries and decide what makes a dictionary "good." You could work with idioms, or do research, writing, or presentations about countries. We suggest that you let the interests of the class lead you a bit. We think "being interested" is a great tool for learning.

FIELD TESTERS' NOTES • • •

1 *The students enjoyed the readings about Ali, Izrail and Faina. The English was easily within their reach, and many of them had experienced the same problems (not understanding the TV) so found it comforting and encouraging to hear the problems expressed by others. My Iraqi student could have substituted his name in Ali's story—he was also an Arabic teacher, and his experience is otherwise identical—which gave the material immediate validity . . .*

Judith Chalkley
Prince Georges County Refugee Training Program
Hyattsville, MD

Good to include a teacher's story!

Andrea Parrella
Adult Learning Program at English High
Jamaica Plain, MA

2. Playing with the Story Language

A. Restating a text in your own words, or paraphrasing, is one way to make sure you understand the essential meaning of a text. Choose one of the Harrisburg stories and reread it. When you understand the story, tell it to a partner. Do you both agree about the content of the story?

Original Text	Paraphrase
I need to go into a different life than my life before. (Izrail)	My life changed. I have to change.
Now people travel to Harrisburg from Russia, Vietnam, Iraq, Ethiopia, and many other places.	People come to Harrisburg from many places.
	IDIOM in your own words

B. Now, below, use simple, clear sentences to paraphrase the story:

_____

_____

_____

_____

_____

_____

_____

_____

_____

C. In his story, Michael Westover uses two common idioms: "they are in the same boat" and "that really wakes them up." Using the story itself to give you clues, paraphrase the idioms. Share your ideas with your partner. Do you agree or disagree about the meaning of the idioms? Do you have similar idioms in your native language?

1. _____

2. _____

---

3. Learning About Each Other: Life Before North America

Izrail said that he needed more English so he could begin a different life than the one he had had before. He had been working as an electrical engineer in Moscow for 47 years. Israil's wife, Faina, had been a neurologist for 40 years before they left Russia.

A. Ask some of your classmates about their lives before they came to North America. Record the answers on the chart. Compare the answers. Do you see any similarities?

Name	How many years did you go to school?	What did you study?	Had you studied English before you came here?	What was your job before?

B. Identify the verb tenses in the paragraph at the top of the page and in the chart that you filled out. Why do you think past time can be expressed in so many ways? What ways do you use to express past time? Share your ideas with the class.

Past Perfect	Past Perfect Continuous
Ali had taught Arabic before he moved to Saudi Arabia.	Michael had been living in Harrisburg before he began teaching.
The past perfect tense shows action that finished before another action in the past. This tense is formed by adding **had** + the **past participle** to the subject.	The past perfect continuous tense shows action that continued for some amount of time before another action in the past. This tense is formed by adding **had + been** + the **present participle** to the subject.

INSTRUCTOR'S JOURNAL

_____

_____

_____

_____

_____

_____

_____

AUTHORS' NOTES • • •

2 Paraphrasing is a higher-order skill that learners need in academic study, on the job, and, perhaps, in explaining homework to their children. Paraphrasing is a complex task that requires reading comprehension, and knowledge of vocabulary and grammar. We think it is important to give learners many opportunities to practice paraphrasing, and later, summarizing both from written and oral language.

A.–B. Using the examples of text and paraphrase, make your own text examples and then ask your learners to paraphrase orally. For instance, you could ask the class to paraphrase some of Mariano's words from Unit 1. Paraphrasing orally and talking with a partner will help the learners to clarify their ideas and words before they write.

C. This activity is open-ended so you and the class can decide what to concentrate on: paraphrasing, conversation, or cultural comparison.

3 **A.–B.** Depending on the level and needs of your class, you may want to review the past perfect and past perfect continuous tenses before the learners begin the grid.

FIELD TESTERS' NOTES • • •

2 *C. Maybe this activity could be more personal. Partners could discuss instances in their lives where these idioms are exemplified.*

Nancy Breese
Petaluma Adult School
Petaluma, CA

3 *I did activity B first because I didn't know how much my new student had studied before, and we had already touched on some time-related grammar—the use of "since" and "for" and "ago" when doing the paraphrasing. All except one of my students have spent time in a camp . . . so we were easily able to use their own experiences as examples of both verb tenses. This was a nice way for me to learn more about their histories. When they moved on to activity A, they were pleased to be able to use the newly acquired grammar in their questions to each other.*

Judith Chalkley
Prince Georges County Refugee Training Program
Hyattsville, MD

4 — Doing It in English: Explaining What We Need

Adriana Ariza had studied microbiology in Colombia before she came to the United States. In her country she had been working in quality control in food. Adriana says she needs to speak English. She studies in Michael Westover's class at Immigration and Refugee Services in Harrisburg, Pennsylvania.

In English there are many ways to express necessity:

I need a job.
I need to work.
I have to study.
I must practice every day.
I've got to speak more.
It's necessary to listen carefully.

Word Formation

I **need** to study.
It's **necessary** to go.
Practice is a **necessity**.

To understand the meaning and the function of words, look at the **roots** and the **affixes**.

A. Why do you need to study English? Work with a small group to write a list of reasons why it is necessary to study English. Share your list with the whole class. Does each group list the same reasons?

_____
_____
_____
_____
_____
_____
_____

5 — Other Voices from North America

A. Think about your school now and before you came to North America. What was the relationship between students and teachers? Do you have that same relationship with your teachers now?

B. Read the story. Keep your questions in mind as you read.

Thu-Thuy Nguyen came to the United States from Vietnam. She studies at Northern Virginia Community College. She lives with her family in Arlington, Virginia.

In some ways teachers are both the same and different than in Vietnam. I can tell you about the differences. In my country, when I was a small child, my father always taught me. So, in Vietnam, teachers are like parents. You have respect for them. In this country it is different because the students go to the school and, after they finish, some of them forget about their teachers. In my country that's not the custom. When I was small, I studied in middle school and I have always remembered that. So, the teacher always keeps the relationship with the students—all of them. The teacher is always proud of them and always helps them if they have difficulties in their lives.

Before I came here, listening to English was very difficult. After that, I went to school and to work and it was very easy to practice speaking and listening. I have a problem and I think other students are like me. They have some problems with reading. You know, sometimes when you read *The Washington Post* or *The New York Times*, you can not read all the words—you always find new words. So I think this is my weakness. I think right now I have to learn new words. When I find a new word, I write it down in a notebook, and I find it in the dictionary. After that, I make a sentence. Also, I have read short stories and after that, I have read novels, because the college always requires students to take English. It's not English As a Second Language and, for the class, you have to read books. So I try to read every day. Right now I am reading *Animal Farm*.

PROVERB

English: First learn politeness, then learn knowledge.

Vietnamese: Tiên học lễ, hậu học văn

INSTRUCTOR'S JOURNAL

_____
_____
_____
_____
_____
_____
_____

Page 24	Correlates with:	Page 25
Workbook: pages 19–20		Activity Masters: page 21

AUTHORS' NOTES • • •

4   Knowing about roots and affixes helps learners construct sentences and expand vocabulary, both of which will enhance their test-taking abilities for standardized tests such as the "Michigan Test" and TOEFL. Page 20 of the *Workbook* gives more information and practice about roots. We recommend integrating word formation practice into the class daily. As new vocabulary pops up, ask students to look for clues to meaning and function.

A. At the high-intermediate level, we think learners need a lot of conversation and that it should be less controlled by the instructor, or even by the assignment, than in lower levels. This activity gives the learners a chance to negotiate in both the small and large group about a topic important to all.

5   **A.** The pre-reading prompts can generate a lot of heartfelt discussion as happened in Alan Shute's class. Many adult learners are trying hard to understand the North American "idea" of education because they have children attending school. Try to solicit parents' comments about school. Do they understand the culture of relationships between students, teachers, and parents? Do they know about parent-teacher conferences? Your class may be the place where parents can find and share knowledge about our educational system.

FIELD TESTERS' NOTES • • •

4   *We talked about roots and affixes using words that are familar to them already (careful–careless, review–inteview). I find students always enjoy learning about this aspect of English because it is solving a puzzle to put together the meaning of new words. I had some interesting answers to Activity A; one of my students said English is necessary for safety. This activity served well as a reinforcement of things we had talked about in a morning job class, as well as an opportunity for students to talk about their own lives and needs.*

Judith Chalkley
Prince Georges County Refugee Training Program
Hyattsville, MD

5   **A.** *This provoked the most extensive reactions from the students. Several students explained how teachers were treated in their cultures and how students behave: In Bangladesh and Vietnam, students stand up when the teacher calls on them and are subject to punishment if their answers do not satisfy the teacher . . . This activity was successful because all the students have experience in their native countries as well as here. For some, there is a considerable difference between educational systems and the roles and responsibililites of teachers and students.*

Alan Shute
Bunker Hill Community College
Boston, MA

Moustafa Kattih is from Syria. He lives in Corpus Christi, Texas. In the future he would like to teach in a university here in the United States. Moustafa studies at the Corpus Christi Literacy Council.

I was a teacher in the high school and college. I taught Arabic literature. I taught about 30 years and then I retired, and I came here to visit my son.

A teacher is a prophet because he makes the human being. Every job makes things: this man sells something, this man makes an electrical machine, this one builds homes, but we build the person. So, in my religion, the best person in the world is one who teaches others because he builds the person. This is from Prophet Mohammed. The soldier kills, the construction worker builds a roof; but in all the world, the teacher is the best person.

The second thing, in all the world, we really love the students. Parents love their kids more than themselves and the teachers love their students more than themselves. The teachers always are very tired because they give from their hearts and not from their arms. I will tell you one sentence: If I went back in my life 40 years, and I was back in high school in 1952, I wouldn't study anything different—only to be a teacher another time.

 Vietnam lies along the South China Sea in Southeast Asia. The Vietnamese people make up approximately 90 percent of the population, but there are many minority groups such as the Chinese, Khmer, Muong, Meo, and Thai. Hundreds of thousands of people died in the Vietnam War, and many thousands emigrated.

Syria is at the eastern edge of the Mediterranean Sea. The capital, Damascus, is over 4,000 years old. Syria has been important throughout its history because it lies along trade routes that link Asia, Africa, and Europe. Most of Syria's more than 15 million people are Muslim Arabs.

---

6 **Think It Over:** The Culture of Education

A. In their stories, Thu-Thuy and Moustafa expressed strong beliefs about students, teachers, and learning. Both used special kinds of language to express intense feeling. Special types of language, such as **metaphors** and **similes,** are called **figures of speech.** Find and list figures of speech from each story. Check your ideas with the class.

Figures of Speech
Alliteration
Metaphor
Overstatement
Paradox
Personification
Simile
Understatement

Similes
Learning English is like making vegetable soup.
Similes compare two unlike things using the words **like** or **as.**

Thu-Thuy:

_____

_____

Moustafa:

_____

_____

B. Think about your own culture. How do people think about students, teachers, and learning? Finish the following phrases with figures of speech or words from your culture.

Teachers are (like) _____.

Children (or students) are (like) _____.

School (or education) is (like) _____.

 C. Compare your sentences with your group and then with the whole class. Are the sentences similar or different? On the computer or using poster board and markers, write the sentences in English and in your native language. Find a place to share your ideas: the entrance to your school, the office, a bulletin board, or maybe an elementary school!

INSTRUCTOR'S JOURNAL

_____

_____

_____

_____

_____

_____

_____

Page 26	**Correlates with:**	**Page 27**
		Workbook: page 22

AUTHORS' NOTES ● ● ●

Thu-Thuy's and Moustafa's expressive stories give further range and depth to the ongoing discussion of learners and teachers. Thu-Thuy talks of her respect for teachers while Moustafa talks about how "teachers love their students."

Here, or in other places throughout the text, learners can find information about their own or classmates' countries and write informational paragraphs. Learners can practice using the public library's information system, card catalogue, or reference desk to find materials. If available, learners could search the Internet for information.

6 **A.** We've found that learners love studying about figures of speech, poetry, and song lyrics. Searching for figures of speech in the stories helps learners focus on the language itself. Similes and metaphors are easy to spot, and serve as a jumping off place for exploring other figures of speech. You could begin with "Dr. Seuss" tongue-twisters for alliteration and Carl Sandburg's "Fog" for personification.

If you have a strongly multilevel class, you can pair the stronger readers with others so they can complete the task together.

B.–C. After students have learned figures of speech or sayings, they can create an evocative and beautiful class project. We've found that, even at the high-intermediate level, learners like to use markers and colored paper to express themselves. Bilingual signs (like the bilingual proverbs shown in the text) reflect pride, both in one's native language and culture and in their growing ability in English.

FIELD TESTERS' NOTES ● ● ●

5–6 *The readings with their figures of speech made it easy for students to generate their own. These two activities were good preparation for the interview activity in Activity 11B. ("Ideas for Action") . . .*

I found all the figures of speech listed to be unnecessary . . . since there weren't examples of each in the stories.

Alan Shute
Bunker Hill Community College
Boston, MA

(7) Doing It in English: Identifying and Suggesting Learning Strategies

A. The students in this unit have written about methods, or strategies, which help them to learn English. List at least three strategies from the stories.

Strategies
The student's strategy was to read the newspaper every day.
A strategy is a specific plan to accomplish a particular goal.

Student	Strategy
_____	_____
_____	_____
_____	_____

B. Do you use any of the above strategies to learn English? Are they effective? Work with your group to brainstorm a complete list of language learning strategies. Try to decide which strategies are most effective for the most students. When you have the final list, ask your teacher which strategy he/she thinks is best. Do you agree or disagree?

PROVERB
English: A book is a friend.
Vietnamese: Sách là một người bạn.

(8) Bringing the Outside In: Movies

A. Watch the movie, *Stand and Deliver*, with your classmates and teacher. Work with a partner to answer the following questions and then talk with the class about the movie.

1. What is happening in the movie?

2. Who are the characters in the movie?

3. What is the setting of the movie (where/when is it)?

4. What is the main idea of the movie?

5. What emotions are expressed in the movie?

6. Is the movie easy or difficult for you to understand? Explain.

B. Is watching a movie a good strategy for learning English? Why or why not? Discuss your answers with the whole class.

C. Work with the class to recommend a list of movies, TV shows, and radio programs that might help students practice English skills.

(9) Journal Writing: Students and Teachers

Choose one of the following topics to write about:

1. Compare your experiences studying English with those of one of the students you've read about. Have your experiences been similar or not? Explain your ideas.

2. Think about teachers here and in your native country. What are the essential characteristics of a good teacher? Explain your ideas.

INSTRUCTOR'S JOURNAL

Page 28	Correlates with:	Page 29
Transparencies: page 6		Workbook: page 24
Workbook: pages 16 and 23		Activity Masters: page 22
Activity Masters: pages 14, 19–22		

AUTHORS' NOTES ● ● ●

7   **A.** This is a good time to review the idea of "strategies." The concept is important in our culture and our learners need to understand, use, and talk about strategies in school, work, and the community. As learners search the stories for strategies, we think they will realize that they have many learning strategies of their own. Some learners may prefer a more traditional classroom—with the teacher explaining the *proper* ways to learn—but we feel this way serves learners' needs best.

      B. You may decide to divide the groups: what strategies are effective inside class and what strategies are effective outside class. Both the *Workbook* pages 16 and 23 and *Activity Masters* page 14 should be completed in connection with this activity. The learners will want your advice. What strategies do you think are best? Why? What strategies do you use for language learning?

8   We like showing *Stand and Deliver* because it has everything: multiculture, easy to understand, good story, good acting, good ending, and it's authentic. Sharing popcorn, laughs, and tears enhances the classroom community. Another excellent movie for intermediate learners is *The Long Walk Home* about the Montgomery bus boycott.

9   Either topic follows a main thread of the unit. *Activity Master* page 22 gives a rationale and advice for journal writing.

FIELD TESTERS' NOTES ● ● ●

7   *We talked about different learning strategies. When I have more time, I will do an activity to follow up Izrail's comment on the difficulty of knowing which are the "proper" definitions. I have the students look up some particularly confusing words, such as "mean," and decide which definition fits in example sentences. If anything, I find my students are too dictionary-prone and I like to encourage them to use other learning strategies.*

Judith Chalkley
Prince Georges County Refugee Training Program
Hyattsville, MD

8   *This would work well. I always show this movie in the "school" unit.*

Nancy Breese
Petaluma Adult School
Petaluma, CA

Reading
About It: Skimming and Scanning for Information

Reading Strategy: Skimming	Reading Strategy: Scanning
Reading titles, headings, introductions and summaries, and bold words can help you understand the general meaning of an article quickly.	Letting your eyes quickly move over the text can help you find specific information that you need, such as: numbers, dates, names, or places.

A. After noting the titles and subtitles of the following article, quickly skim it. Write the main idea of the article in two or three sentences.

_____

_____

_____

_____

 B. Compare your sentence with your classmates' sentences. Do you agree or disagree about the main idea of the article?

CORPUS CHRISTI LITERACY COUNCIL PROGRAMS
"OPEN WINDOWS TO THE WORLD"

The Corpus Christi Literacy Council is located at 4044 Greenwood with office space in the Greenwood Library. Regular office hours are 8:00 A.M. to 5:00 P.M., Monday through Friday.

ONE-ON-ONE TUTORS

Volunteers are trained and certified in a sixteen (16) hour Workshop conducted by certified Tutor Trainers to teach adult students to speak, read, and write the English language. Upon certification, tutors are assigned to students, seventeen years of age or older, reading below a fifth grade competency level or who do not speak the English Language.

The majority of tutoring sessions are conducted at public tutoring sites. There are sixty-nine (69) locations within the Corpus Christi City limits as well as in the Corpus Christi Literacy Council's headquarters. CCLC continues to solicit and train an average of one hundred thirty-five (135) tutors each year to be matched with students in an effort to help with the tremendous need.

Individuals interested in receiving literacy assistance are evaluated by the CCLC to determine current reading level and the ability to speak English conversationally. After the initial evaluation, an application is filed until the individual can be matched with a certified tutor.

The only requirements for a participant are that he/she does not speak English or speaks English in a limited capacity, reads on or below a fifth grade level, is not enrolled in a public school, and is at least seventeen (17) years of age.

TUTOR TRAINING

The Corpus Christi Literacy Council provides Tutor Training to local groups and agencies as well as neighboring cities who request training.

Volunteers are trained and certified in a sixteen (16) hour Workshop conducted by qualified Tutor Trainers. Upon certification, tutors are able to teach students to speak, read, and write the English language.

A person interested in becoming a tutor must be seventeen (17) years of age or older and attend a certification workshop. For more information contact CCLC at 857-5896.

PROJECT-ADVANCE

Project Advance is a classroom instruction program that teaches adult basic literacy instruction. Students attend classes twice a week for six months or approximately 100 hours of instruction. Class sessions are held January through June and July through December. Approximately twenty (20) students are served in each session.

The goal of this program is to enable the participants to increase their reading and writing skills to about a fifth grade competency level. Upon reaching this goal, students are referred to higher level education agencies.

MICROREAD

The MicroRead program is conducted through a partnership grant funded with Job Training Partnership monies. This program is conducted at Del Mar College West Campus and the C.C. Literacy Council classroom. MicroRead is a mixture of computer-assisted and classroom instruction. Depending on the current year's funds, 60 to 100 participants are served each year.

Components of the program include ESL, math, basic literacy, and occupational skills enhancement activities. Participants who qualify for JTPA assistance and are language barriered, nonreaders, and/or reading below a 7.0 grade level are eligible for this program.

Participants are enrolled for forty-seven (47) weeks receiving 100 hours of computer-assisted instruction, 100 of literacy and math instruction combined, and 24 hours of occupational skills training.

C. Quickly scan the article again to answer the following questions:

1. What are the office hours of the Corpus Christi Literacy Council?

_____

2. How many volunteers does the CCLV train every year?

_____

3. What is the minimum age to be a tutor?

_____

4. How many students are served each session in PROJECT-ADVANCE?

_____

5. How many hours of computer-assisted instruction are MicroRead participants offered?

_____

INSTRUCTOR'S JOURNAL

_____

_____

_____

_____

_____

_____

_____

Page 30	Correlates with:	Page 31
Transparencies: page 6		Transparencies: page 6
Workbook: page 21		Workbook: page 21
Activity Masters: page 16		Activity Masters: page 16

AUTHORS' NOTES ● ● ●

10 **A.** Ask the learners a series of questions about *skimming* and *scanning* to see how familiar they are with these strategies. *What do these words mean? When should you use skimming or scanning? Are these methods useful?* Probably some members of your class are familiar with these reading techniques, so they can help explain them to the others. You might demonstrate the original active verb meanings of the words (for ex: skimming the cream off the milk, and scanning the horizon) to illustrate the more conceptual use of the words.

    B. Some learners may get bogged down in the length, vocabulary, and content of the article. However, the main idea of the article is simple, so some will find it easily. As they share their answers with others, the technique will seem less onerous. To help her class to understand, Judith Chalkley suggested that "they (the learners) do these things themselves when reading a magazine in their own language." Our learners bring many skills and strategies with them into our classes. Sometimes, we need to remind them that these skills and strategies can be used in English, also.

    C. If learners have found Parts A and B challenging, save this task for another day or for homework.

Skimming and scanning are strategies that become increasingly important as learners prepare to enter academic study. Learners must read actively and quickly to perform well on standardized tests including the GED. If you gather a collection of articles of varying subject, length, and difficulty, learners can practice these skills as much as they want. Partners could read the same article and discuss the main idea and specific information in class. Or, the articles could provide optional homework.

FIELD TESTERS' NOTES ● ● ●

10 *I spent about twenty minutes introducing the words "skim" and "scan." A number of students have some medical background and so "scan" was familiar. Only three students were able to answer questions about the main ideas in the article. They were more successful with the scanning questions, fortunately . . . The students who were comfortable with these activities have a high educational level and understood the helpfulness of these techniques in studying.*

Judith Chalkley
Prince Georges County Refugee Training Program
Hyattsville, MD

Action: Educational Opportunities in the Community

A. Find information about educational opportunities in your area. Work with your class to make a chart or bulletin board. Include information about times, places, cost, and requirements.

> Although Humberto Gonzales runs his own company, he finds time to teach at the Corpus Christi Literacy Council. Humberto believes that respecting the adult learner is necessary and important.

PROVERB
English: To learn is a gift from God, but to teach is a calling.
Spanish: Aprender es un don, pero enseñar es un apostolado.

B. Interview one of your classmates or someone outside the class. Ask the following questions, plus one of your own. Compare the answers with the rest of the class.

Describe your favorite teacher (in the past or now). Explain the reasons why this teacher is special.

_____

_____

What qualities make a good teacher? Why?

_____

_____

What responsibilities for learning belong with the teacher and with the learner?

_____

_____

_____

_____

Your question: _____

_____

_____

32 •••

:12: Options for
Learning: Using Strategies Outside Class

A. What strategies do you want to use for studying English outside of class? Check (✔) your answers. Add others if you wish.

	Already Do	Want to Do	Not Interested
Find a conversation partner to practice speaking and listening.	_____	_____	_____
Volunteer in the community to practice language skills.	_____	_____	_____
Read the newspaper every day.	_____	_____	_____
Write in a journal every day.	_____	_____	_____
Other? _____	_____	_____	_____

:13: ## Looking Back

Think about your learning. Complete this form. Then tell the class your ideas.

A. The most useful thing I learned in this unit was _____

_____

B. I would still like to learn _____.

C. I learned the most by working

_____ alone. _____ with a partner. _____ with a group.

D. The activity I liked best was 1 2 3 4 5 6 7 8 9 10 11 12

because _____.

E. The activity I liked least was 1 2 3 4 5 6 7 8 9 10 11 12

because _____.

••• 33

INSTRUCTOR'S JOURNAL

_____

_____

_____

_____

_____

_____

_____

_____

Page 32	Correlates with:	Page 33
Workbook: page 21		**Activity Masters: pages 19–22**
Activity Masters: pages 15, 17		

AUTHORS' NOTES ● ● ●

11 **A.** This "Ideas for Action" provides the class the chance to practice skills while finding information important to them all. Many areas offer a bewildering array of educational opportunities, with differing requirements, clientele, schedules, and costs. Gathering and organizing information will help some learners to clarify their goals: *What programs can I afford? What times can I attend? What kind of education, English proficiency, or documentation do I need?* It might be helpful to turn back to "Reading About It" on pages 30–31, to see what kind of programs one agency provides in Corpus Christi.

If you live in an area with many programs, see if the class wants to produce an informational pamphlet to share the information with other classes and programs.

B. If it's feasible, try to have the learners interview someone outside of class. Learners may gather some fascinating stories (interview a local school, church, or government official, a musician, a poet) to compare with their own and to share with the class. Besides, the formality of interviewing an unfamiliar person is excellent practice for real interview situations—for jobs or school. Before the interviews begin, brainstorm a list of appropriate (and inappropriate) possible questions. Assure learners that they can ask several of their own questions.

12 In Unit 2 "Options for Learning," learners can choose which strategies they want to use to increase their English skills. Each of these four options requires practice over time. After handing out *Activity Masters* of what learners "Want to Do," set up a process for them to report back to you and the class. You could make a chart, or ask for students to give weekly oral or written summaries.

13 "Looking Back" is itself a way to help learners become accustomed to thinking about their learning goals and to realize that they are responsible for their learning. We've found that through the course of a class, learners get used to this reflection, and come to expect it and value it.

FIELD TESTERS' NOTES ● ● ●

11 ***B.*** *This activity generated a list of good teacher qualities and student/teacher responsibilities. None of the students generated their own questions. Although I often do this in classes, I haven't yet done it very much with these students, it only being the third week of class.*

Alan Shute
Bunker Hill Community College
Boston, MA

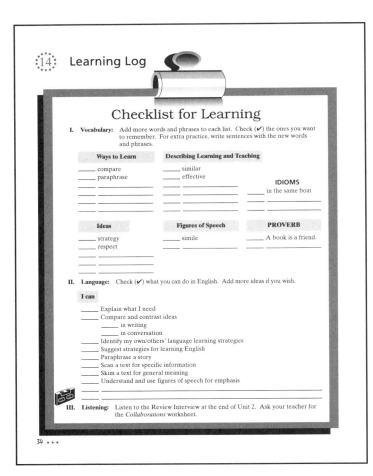

Checklist for Learning

I. Vocabulary: Add more words and phrases to each list. Check (✔) the ones you want to remember. For extra practice, write sentences with the new words and phrases.

Ways to Learn	Describing Learning and Teaching	
_____ compare	_____ similar	
_____ paraphrase	_____ effective	**IDIOMS**
_____	_____	_____ in the same boat
_____	_____	
_____	_____	

Ideas	Figures of Speech	PROVERB
_____ strategy	_____ simile	_____ A book is a friend.
_____ respect	_____	_____
_____		
_____		
_____		

II. Language: Check (✔) what you can do in English. Add more ideas if you wish.

I can

_____ Explain what I need
_____ Compare and contrast ideas
    _____ in writing
    _____ in conversation
_____ Identify my own/others' language learning strategies
_____ Suggest strategies for learning English
_____ Paraphrase a story
_____ Scan a text for specific information
_____ Skim a text for general meaning
_____ Understand and use figures of speech for emphasis
_____
_____

III. Listening: Listen to the Review Interview at the end of Unit 2. Ask your teacher for the *Collaborations* worksheet.

AUTHOR'S NOTES • • •

14 We think that as your class progresses, learners will be pleased with the quality and quantity they are learning. The structure and language of the "Checklist for Learning" also provides learners with ways to express what they need to study further.

For Part III, the Review Interview, you will need to pass out copies of *Activity Masters,* page 23 and play the interview portion of the Unit 2 Audiotape.

FIELD TESTERS' NOTES • • •

Part II This is good. It reminds the students that they do go away with something <u>real</u>.

Nancy Breese
Petaluma Adult School
Petaluma, CA

INSTRUCTOR'S JOURNAL

Page 34	Correlates with:
Audiotape	
Workbook: pages 25–26	
Activity Masters: page 23	
Assessment Program	

Unit 3

Dating and Marriage in Washington, D.C.

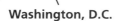

Washington, D.C. is the capital of the United States. In 1790 Congress gave permission for a site on the Potomac River to be chosen for a new capital city. Maryland and Virginia gave land for the city. This area was centrally located in what was then the United States. The capital was named the District of Columbia after Christopher Columbus and the city was called Washington to honor George Washington, the first president of the United States. People from all over the country and all over the world go there to study, work, and live. Millions of tourists come every year to visit the Capitol, the White House, and Washington's famous monuments and museums.

Washington, D.C.

Sandeep Bagla and Monisha Sehgal's Stories

A. What do you know about American dating and marriage customs? How are American dating and marriage customs different and similar to customs in your country?

B. Read the stories. Compare marriage and dating customs of India to your country.

India is the second most populous country in the world with 937,000,000 people. It has about 24 major languages including Hindi, which is the primary language. India has a rich ancient culture dating back 4,000 years. It is the birthplace of Hinduism and Buddhism, two of the world's great religions.

Sandeep Bagla was born in New York. His parents emigrated to the United States from India. Monisha Sehgal was born in California and has lived in the United States, Italy, and India where her parents are from. They are students at George Washington University in Washington, D.C.

Sandeep Bagla:

My parents are originally from northern India but I grew up in New York. I have two older sisters and they spent their first five to eight years in India. Then my family moved here. My parents were raised in India and they instilled in us their values on dating and marriage. In a sense my sisters paved the way for me because my parents are more liberal with me.

My oldest sister was never allowed to go out on dates because when my parents first came here they were very strict. My other sister wanted to go out on dates and my parents tried to be a little more open with her. Then I started dating, but when I was in the ninth grade they found out I was seeing a girl who was two years older than me. They hated this and they forbade me to see her anymore.

For the next two years I didn't talk to my parents. I would come home from school, eat dinner, go to my room to do school work and then go to bed. It was horrible because we didn't have a relationship for two years. After two years they began to give in a little and I also gave in. They realized that for me and my friends, dating did not mean marriage.

> **IDIOMS**
> paved the way
> go out on dates
> find out
> catch on
> give in
> play the field

During those two years they had a lot of opportunities to talk to their friends about what their kids were doing so they were slowly catching on to what dating meant here. At the same time, I quietly accepted more of their ideas.

I see now that dating should not take away from anything else. Education is my main goal. Dating is more of a serious thing for me and I think my relationships have been more serious than many of my friends' relationships.

Even though my parents are more open, they still would not be happy if I just went out on casual dates with lots of girls. In other words, playing the field is not acceptable. So we both changed. Five years ago when I asked my parents if I could go out on a date my mother said no. When I asked her if she knew what a date was, she said no and she didn't want to know. Now they are more accepting and I can talk to them about Monisha. Now they are more interested in what I did on a date than the fact that I went on a date. You know how kids want their parents to be their friends? Well, it is becoming more like that.

> If you were in Sandeep's situation what would you have done?
> If you were Sandeep's parent, what would you have done?

Monisha Sehgal:

If I were raised in the area of India where my parents are from, I would not be dating. If I did date, it would be to the person I was going to marry. There would be no other person. My cousins who live in India don't even think about dating and their marriages are arranged. They always ask me about dating customs here. They tell me that they think it is so weird that people can have several boyfriends or girlfriends before they get married.

> **IDIOMS**
> casual flings

In India girls start getting proposals somewhere between the ages of 16 and 18, depending on the family. Usually by the time a girl is 20 she knows when she will get married. The guys are generally three or four years older than the girls, so that they are established in work and settled.

My parents have already received proposals for me. They don't say much to me because they are liberal that way, but they do think that I should be looking forward to marriage instead of just having casual flings with different boys.

Compared to many of my friends who are completely American, I refrain from just dating anyone. I am looking for a long term commitment but many of my friends are not that serious. They say that they are still in college and they don't have to worry about it. They say that they have the rest of their lives to think about marriage.

> Monisha is looking for a long term commitment but her friends are not as serious. Who do you agree with?

INSTRUCTOR'S JOURNAL

Page 36	Correlates with:	Page 37
Transparency: page 8		Audiotape: Story on tape
Audiotape: Story on tape		Workbook: pages 28–29
		Activity Masters: page 26

AUTHORS' NOTES • • •

The stories in this unit focus on dating and marriage customs in the United States. We hear the perspectives of young people who moved to this country as young children. They tell about the clash of cultures—the old and the new—in their homes. In addition, the issue of multicultural relationships is raised in the interview with the Almanzas. We have included a variety of activities in this unit to bring out the various themes of love, romance, dating, and marriage.

1 The photo transparency of Sandeep and Monisha is a good starting point for discussion. Use the questions at the bottom of the transparency to involve learners in the topic.

Following a discussion of the pre-reading questions, learners should have a chance to read the stories silently so they can read at their own pace. We suggest that learners read the stories without stopping to look up words in a dictionary as this interruption detracts from the feeling of the piece and makes it more difficult to follow the ideas.

You can let learners read both stories before discussing the questions or you can read and discuss the first story before proceeding to the next.

Students will enjoy listening to the tape as they follow along in their books. If building listening skills is important to your students, you can have them listen to the tape before they read the stories themselves.

Sandeep and Monisha are young, perfectly fluent speakers of English. Therefore their speech is very idiomatic. Learners love to be introduced to idioms and these would be good words to put in their "Learning Log" in the *Workbook*.

FIELD TESTERS' NOTES • • •

1 *With the stories, the students looked at the photographs, read the brief bios, and discussed the idioms. They were intrigued by the information about the countries and were especially impressed by the statistics about India particularly when we compared its population of 937,000,000 with the 260,000,000 of the United States.*

All the students could easily identify with Sandeep's situation. Even our most senior student, a rather reserved middle-aged man, said with a big smile, "I never listened to my parents!"

With regard to the boxed questions, it was interesting that at first the men replied easily to the questions about Sandeep and the women to the questions about Monisha. But when I rephrased the questions, trying to involve the whole group in each one, they discovered how much they have in common with Sandeep and with each other.

Linda Nachinoff
Brookline Adult and Community Education Program
Brookline, MA

2 Playing with the Story

A. Listen to part of Sandeep's story. Write the missing words.

Even though my _____ are more open, they still

_____ not be happy if I just _____ out

on casual dates _____ lots of girls. In other

_____, playing the field is not acceptable. So we both

changed. Five years ago when I _____ my parents if I

could go _____ on a date my mother _____ no. When I asked

her if she _____ what a date was, she said no and she _____

want to know. Now they are more _____ and I can talk to them

_____ Monisha. Now they are more _____ in what I did on a

date _____ the fact that I went on a date. You know how kids want their

_____ to be their friends? Well, it is _____ more like that.

Reported Speech
Quote / Reported Speech
He said, "I **need** to study English." — He said he **needed** to study English.
She said, "I **wrote** a letter." — She said that she **had written** a letter.
Reported speech tells what someone said without using a direct quote. **Direct quotes** in the simple past or present perfect can be changed to past perfect in reported speech.

B. Underline the sentences with reported speech in each story.

C. Change the reported speech to direct quotes from Monisha's story.

1. They tell me that they think it is so weird that people can have several boyfriends or girlfriends before they get married.

   They told me, "We think it is so weird that people can have several boyfriends
   or girlfriends before they get married."

2. They say that they are still in college and they don't have to worry about it.

   _____

3. They say that they have the rest of their lives to think about marriage.

   _____

3 Learning About Each Other: Finding a Mate

A. Learn about a classmate's country. Complete the first part of the table about your country. Then, interview your partner about marriage and dating customs in their country.

	Your country	Your partner's country
1. How do couples become acquainted?		
2. Do people date?		
3. At what age do men and women begin dating?		
4. Where do people go on dates?		
5. At what age do people usually get married?		
6. Is it acceptable for a man or a woman to stay single?		
7. Are marriages arranged?		

Expressing Generalities
Generally, men ask women for a date. — Men **generally** ask women for a date.
Usually, men ask women for a date. — Men **usually** ask women for a date.
Generally and *usually* can be placed at the beginning of the sentence or before the verb.
In general, men ask women for a date. — **As a rule** men ask women for a date.
As a rule and *in general* also express a typical occurrence.

B. Write sentences about your partner's country that express generalities about dating and marriage. Show your partner.

_____

_____

_____

_____

INSTRUCTOR'S JOURNAL

Page 38	Correlates with:	Page 39
Audiotape		**Workbook: page 30**
Workbook: page 30		**Activity Masters: page 27–28**
Activity Masters: page 29		

AUTHORS' NOTES ● ● ●

2   You may want learners to try to fill in as much of the cloze as they can before listening to the tape. At this level they should check the text for their own errors. A discussion of why some errors were made engages learners in analyzing and assessing their own work.

In Parts B and C the learners are working with quotes and reported speech. We suggest that you give learners plenty of examples of how to use quotation marks and how to change quotes into reported speech. The exercises in the *Workbook* and *Activity Masters* provide learners with more opportunities to use reported speech in other contexts.

3   Students always enjoy learning about each other's countries and cultures. If your situation is similar to Janine Tabor's, you might want to turn this into a whole class discussion followed by the "Pair Off" activity in the *Activity Masters* that deals with opinions on dating and marriage. You can still follow up with the exercise in expressing generalities.

Following the conversation grid, learners can practice expressing generalities by taking the information that their partner gave them and making general statements about it. Cynthia Fong had a very nice way of connecting these two exercises.

FIELD TESTERS' NOTES ● ● ●

3   *The students enjoyed "Learning About Each Other." However, since 98 percent of the students in class are from the same country, Mexico, this exercise probably would have been more interesting and successful in a less homogeneous group.*

Janine Tabor
Salinas Adult School
Salinas, CA

I wrote all the names of the students' countries on the blackboard and pointing to each country, I had "interviewers" report in general statements some of the information they had learned from their partners. Some of the most interesting differences were in the ages of marriage and the acceptability of staying single.

Cindy Fong
Bunker Hill Community College
Boston, MA

4   Another Story from
Washington, D.C.: An Interview with the Almanzas

Dorothy and Marcos Almanza live in the Washington D.C. area. Dorothy is from the United States and teaches English as a second language. Marcos is from Bolivia and is a construction worker.

A. How easy or difficult do you think it would be to have a bilingual or bicultural relationship? Do you know couples who come from different cultures or have different first languages?

B. Read the story. Circle the words you want to remember.

Dorothy

I think language plays a big part when we are spending time with his family. I know very little Quechua and Spanish. I try to understand the conversation and I understand a little but I don't want Marcos to feel he has to translate all the time. That can interfere with the time he is spending with his family.

Marcos

Sometimes language plays a role in our relationship. For example, when she is having a conversation with someone about books they are reading, I can't always get into the conversation. I didn't grow up in this culture and I didn't read any of these books so it can be kind of hard to participate in the conversation. When that happens I just slip out.

IDIOMS
play a role
a little bit
slip out
spend time with
get a point across

Dorothy

When we are having an argument sometimes it gets frustrating trying to get our points across. We might start an argument and then realize we weren't really disagreeing at all because we were just having some little misunderstanding about language. After talking for a while, one of us will say something like, "Oh, that's what you meant!"

I think we are a lot more patient with each other than in the beginning. Now we recognize that many of the differences that we used to see as being cultural differences are just the way we are as people. Sometimes in the beginning we would say to ourselves "Oh that's cultural." We would use it as an excuse. We don't do that anymore. Now we try to work things out instead of using that excuse.

Bolivia is located in the central part of South America. The population of Bolivia is almost 8,000,000. About one third of the country lies more than a mile above sea level in the Andes Mountains. From the Andes the land stretches to the Amazon lowlands. Bolivia is a landlocked country. It shares control of Lake Titicaca, the highest navigable lake in the world, with Peru.

C. Discuss the following questions with a small group.

1. How do language and cultural differences play a role in the Almanza's relationship?

2. Have you ever had a misunderstanding or funny experience because you didn't understand someone's language or culture or someone didn't understand yours?

5   Journal Writing

Choose one of the following to write about in your journal.

1. Describe a conflict that you had with your parents. What was it about? How was it resolved?

2. Tell about a date you or someone you know had.

3. Tell about a misunderstanding you or someone you know had because of language.

INSTRUCTOR'S JOURNAL

AUTHORS' NOTES ● ● ●

4   The *Transparency* shows two families, the
Almanzas and the Schaeffers. The husbands and wives
are from different countries and have different first
languages. Use the questions at the bottom of the
transparency for pre-reading discussion. For an
additional pre-reading activity, you may want to have
learners predict what they think the reading will be
about.

   The idioms in the box can be discussed prior to or
after the reading. If done after the reading, ask learners
to guess the meaning of the expressions by looking at
contextual clues.

5   The journal writing topics follow the themes
introduced in the three stories in the student text. If
learners want to write about a different subject relating
to the theme, they should be encouraged to do so.

FIELD TESTERS' NOTES ● ● ●

4   *The introductory questions to the Almanzas' story
provoked an unexpectedly lively and revealing
discussion of bilingual and bicultural relationships. All
the students participated and there was much laughter
and amazement at how many personal experiences they
had in common.*

Linda Nachinoff
Brookline Adult and Community Education Program
Brookline, MA

5   *Almost all the students responded enthusiastically
to the first question in journal writing, while a few wrote
about the language misunderstanding.*

Linda Nachinoff
Brookline Adult and Community Education Program
Brookline, MA

6 Sharing Ideas: The Perfect Mate

Sincerity is really important. Also flexibility—the ability to adapt is important.

A person should be patient and have a good sense of humor.

A person should be a good companion and somebody you can trust. She's told me her closest secrets and I've told her mine. I never think twice that it's going to go anywhere afterwards.

They should be someone you can talk to and someone who is always there for you.

A. In a small group look at the following characteristics. Put a check ✔ on those that are very important to you or your partners.

The perfect mate should:	You	(name)	(name)	(name)
1. have a good education	_____	_____	_____	_____
2. have a lot of money	_____	_____	_____	_____
3. have a sense of humor	_____	_____	_____	_____
4. be patient	_____	_____	_____	_____
5. be handsome or beautiful	_____	_____	_____	_____
6. have a good job	_____	_____	_____	_____
7. be from my culture	_____	_____	_____	_____
8. be flexible	_____	_____	_____	_____
9. be trustworthy	_____	_____	_____	_____
10. know how to cook	_____	_____	_____	_____
11. _____	_____	_____	_____	_____
12. _____	_____	_____	_____	_____
13. _____	_____	_____	_____	_____
14. _____	_____	_____	_____	_____

Learning Strategy
By sharing ideas we expand our knowledge and awareness of differing opinions.

B. Share your information with the rest of the class. In general, what were the most important characteristics?

_____
_____
_____
_____

INSTRUCTOR'S JOURNAL

_____
_____
_____
_____
_____
_____
_____

AUTHORS' NOTES ● ● ●

6 The first page highlights quotes from the different storytellers of this unit. We recommend you discuss these quotes and let learners in your class react to them. Following this, read through the list relating to the perfect mate and brainstorm four other characteristics that they would like to include. You may find that they offer more than four and that's fine. Just have students copy them onto another paper.

The *Workbook* activity focuses on describing people. If you like, you can work on the first part of the *Workbook* page, before the grid in the text, to generate more ways of describing people. If this topic has been met with a spirited discussion and you feel they would like to continue to work on it, the paragraph writing on page 32 of the *Workbook* can be changed and learners can write about their ideas of a perfect mate.

Part B gives learners a chance to synthesize the results of their group's opinions and write general statements. Review with them how to write general statements.

FIELD TESTERS' NOTES ● ● ●

6 *The Perfect Mate discussion was very animated and the students were completely involved. Some students needed definitions of "flexibility" and "adapt" but in general the difficulty level of this activity was perfect for my advanced level ESL students. We did this activity in groups of four, two men and two women, to ensure that everybody was well represented and not outnumbered.*

Janine Tabor
Salinas Adult School
Salinas, CA

7 Doing It
in English: Making, Accepting, and Declining Invitations

> I was wondering if you'd like to go to a movie?
>
> Tomorrow evening?
>
> That's a great idea. When?
>
> Okay. How about at 8?
>
> How about going out to eat?
>
> I'm sorry, I can't. I have to study. Maybe some other time.

Write in the calendar below three things you have to do this week. Next, begin inviting your classmates to participate in an activity with you. If your classmate **can** join you, add the name and activity to your calendar. Fill the entire week with activities.

Sunday	Monday	Tuesday	Wednesday	Thursday	Friday	Saturday
A.M.:	A.M.:	A.M.:	A.M.:	A.M.:	A.M.:	A.M.:
P.M.:	P.M.:	P.M.:	P.M.:	P.M.:	P.M.:	P.M.:

Making and Responding to Invitations	
Do you want + infinitive: Would you be interested in + gerund:	Do you want **to do** something tomorrow? Would you be interested in **going** to the movies?
Accepting an invitation:	I'd like that. That sounds nice.
Declining an invitation	I'd love to, but . . . I'm afraid I can't because . . . *It is considered polite to give an explanation.*

8 Bringing the Outside In: Wedding Ceremonies

Teach the class about your country. Bring in photos or traditional symbols of an engagement or wedding from your country. Share them with the class.

An engagement is a period of time that begins when two people decide to get married. Often the man gives the woman a diamond ring as a symbol of their engagement. During this time they plan their wedding. The bride usually wears a white dress and veil. The groom wears a formal suit called a tuxedo. The couple chooses two people to be witnesses of the marriage—the maid of honor and the best man. The wedding is usually followed by a party called a reception. One tradition is for the bride and groom to cut the wedding cake and feed each other a piece.

Alan Geralnick and Adrienne Eng are from the United States. They were married in Brooklyn, New York.

This wedding took place in Hartford, Connecticut. The couple had a traditional Lao Buddhist ceremony after a Western ceremony in a church.

INSTRUCTOR'S JOURNAL

Page 44	Correlates with:	Page 45
Workbook: page 33 Activity Masters: pages 31, 34		Workbook: pages 34–35

AUTHORS' NOTES ● ● ●

7   The practice of making, accepting, and declining invitations is included in this chapter because these activities are often associated with dating. However, there are many other occasions for invitations so the focus of the activities in the *Student Book, Workbook,* and *Activity Masters* deals with invitations in a general way.

We suggest that you talk about different social situations and different registers one can encounter and how the language and tone can change. For example, declining a friend's invitation to go to the movies and declining an invitation for a first date require different approaches. The former would generally be less formal then the latter. Learners are often very curious about the customs associated with asking someone on a date but they are also concerned about the proper way to ask and respond to other invitations.

An extended activity would be to have partners role play different situations where one person extends an invitation and the other responds. Possible situations:

- Ask a co-worker to go somewhere on the weekend
- Invite a friend to play sports (volleyball, baseball, etc.)
- Ask someone for a first or second date
- Invite a new co-worker to go to lunch

8   Learners should be encouraged to bring in photographs, or other things relating to engagements and weddings in their countries. Learners enjoy sharing the symbols of this happy time and they are very interested in learning about each other's customs. The reading in the *Workbook* extends this discussion as it deals with changing trends in our society. As a follow-up, they can discuss if or how the customs are changing in their society.

FIELD TESTERS' NOTES ● ● ●

7   *I did a "Find Someone Who" activity to supplement this to allow for more oral practice.*

Find someone who . . .

wants to go dancing	would like to go swimming next week
wants to see a movie	wants to play volleyball

1. *Each box contains one phrase:*
   "wants to go dancing"
   "would like to go swimming next week"
2. *Students change the phrases to questions and everyone asks each other. When a student accepts your invitation, you write the name on the line. The first to fill the boxes wins. The goal can also be to get all declines. It also works well if you don't make it competitive.*

Cindy Fong
Bunker Hill Community College
Boston, MA

8   *I brought in a video of my cousin's wedding and a clip of the cake feeding. It was great, the students were happy that I was sharing my family with them and it prompted students to bring in their videos (a wedding in Vietnam and one in the Dominican Republic).*

Cindy Fong
Bunker Hill Community College
Boston, MA

A. Read the poem and discuss the questions.

> **THE NIGHT HAS A THOUSAND EYES**
>
> The night has a thousand eyes,
>   And the day but one;
> Yet the light of the bright world dies
>   With the dying sun.
>
> The mind has a thousand eyes,
>   The heart but one;
> Yet the light of the whole life dies
>   When love is done.
>
> *Francis William Bourdillon*

Francis William Bourdillon was a British poet. He lived from 1852 to 1921.

1. What do the thousand eyes of the night represent?
2. What do the thousand eyes of the mind represent?
3. How does the poem make you feel?
4. Why do you think the poet wrote this poem?

Learning Strategy

Interpreting is explaining what something means to you. Individuals may not have the same interpretation of a poem. When you share your interpretation, give reasons for your ideas.

Reading Strategy

Poetry often uses images to communicate ideas and feelings. As a reader, use these feelings to help you interpret the poet's message.

B. What images do you see when you read this poem? Draw a picture of the poem. Share it with the class.

C. A *cinquain* is a five-line poem. The cinquains on this page have a grammatical structure. Each line needs a specific type of word.

> Line 1 = 1 NOUN
> Line 2 = 2 ADJECTIVES
> Line 3 = 3 VERBS with *ing* endings
> Line 4 = 1 COMPLETE SENTENCE
> Line 5 = 1 NOUN (different from the first)

> Family
> warm, close
> gathering, trusting, loving
> Family is the smallest, tightest group of people.
> Dinner
>
> *Chiyo Yasuda*

Chiyo Yasuda studies English at the Garnet Adult Center in Charleston, West Virginia.

> Friend
> funny, smart
> loving, sharing, caring
> Life is sweet with you at my side.
> Dave
>
> *Donna Moss*

Donna is one of the authors of this book. She teaches English in Arlington, Virginia. David is a computer specialist in Washington, D.C.

D. Brainstorm with the class possible topics for a cinquain.

E. Write a cinquain. Share it with the class.

INSTRUCTOR'S JOURNAL

Page 46
Activity Masters: page 32

Correlates with:

Page 47
Workbook: page 36
Activity Masters: pages 30, 33

46 • • •

AUTHORS' NOTES . . .

9   Longfellow said, "All that is best in the great poets of all countries is not what is national in them, but what is universal." When one thinks about love, romance, and marriage one tends to remember at the very least, snatches of songs and poems. For this reason, we have included poetry in this unit. Learners explore images and interpret an author's words.

The "language of love" can be very complex. You may want to consider looking at the lyrics to popular songs that your students are hearing on the radio every day. Discuss the idioms and images in modern verse and then compare them to the images in Bourdillon's poem and the Shakespearean sonnet in the *Activity Masters*.

Before learners open their books, put the title of the Bourdillon poem on the board. Ask learners what they think it means. Ask them to predict what the poem will be about. Let the class read the poem silently and then we recommend you read it aloud.

Part B allows learners to explore their feelings and the images of the poem in another medium. We have found that even learners at this level like to get out the crayons once in a while and express themselves in a visual manner. If you prefer, you can have learners focus on the images and draw whatever comes to their minds as they hear you read the poem. If you do the drawing activity this way, then do not have the students read the poem first—let them hear it several times, draw as they listen and then read it for themselves.

In "Options for Learning," they can learn the lyrics to an old folksong and be challenged by reading a sonnet by Shakespeare.

Part C introduces the cinquain. Cinquains work well with ESL students because they are very structured. Powerful, beautiful poems are created in this simple structure. In the *Activity Masters,* the class project extends this creative writing component by asking learners to create a class book of poetry.

FIELD TESTERS' NOTES . . .

9   *I explained very briefly what a poem is and how it uses language. I asked the students to read the poem silently once or twice and then I read it aloud. When the students were asked the first two questions they took great pleasure in answering them correctly and then several students eagerly explained what the last two lines meant to them. This brief encounter with a moving poem had a great impact on most of the class. The "why" of this lies in the power of poetry and in this particular poem and the class's readiness for the experience.*

Linda Nachinoff
Brookline Adult and Community Education Program
Brookline, MA

My best cinquains were produced by the snowstorms of the last couple of years. We had an opportunity to share a common experience about which they had strong feelings. They really wanted the new vocabulary about the event (blizzard, sleet, accumulation). Some of the language was practical, but because of their personal experiences about the weather, the cinquains translated their feelings very well. And what is poetry supposed to be but an original way of looking at something ordinary?

Pat Thurston
Arlington Education and Employment Program (REEP)
Arlington, VA

10   Think It Over: Finding Solutions

In a small group read and discuss **one** of the following situations. What are the problems? What advice would you give to the people? What might happen if they follow your advice? Report your ideas to the class.

1. Ana is from El Salvador but lives and works in Toronto. Ana's daughter, Elisa, is seventeen years old. Elisa met a young man named Alfredo in her chemistry class in high school. Alfredo has asked her to go to the movies on Friday night. Ana tells her daughter she can not go because Ana does not know Alfredo or his family. Elisa is angry and tells her mother that all her friends go on dates and that she is not a baby. She says that she will find a way to go out with Alfredo.

2. Hung and Ginny are getting married. Hung is from Vietnam and wants to have a traditional Vietnamese wedding. Ginny is from the United States. She wants a small civil wedding with only the immediate family members attending. She wants to save the money for their honeymoon.

3. Ali and Rachida are from Morocco. They are living in the United States. Ali studies at the university and Rachida lives with her parents and works in a bank. They are in love and plan to get married. Ali wants to return to Morocco when he graduates. He wants to start a business. Rachida loves her work in the United States and wants to remain in the United States close to her family.

> **Learning Strategy**
>
> Ask youself what consequences a solution to a problem might have.

Problems
_____
_____

Solutions	Consequences
_____	_____
_____	_____

Advice with *should* and *ought to*

She **should call** the doctor.   He **ought to practice** English everyday.

Should and **ought to** are used to express advice. They are followed by the simple form of the verb.

11   Options for Learning: English at Home

A. What tasks do you want to perform in English? Check (✔) your answers. Add other tasks if you wish.

	Can Do	Want to Learn	Not Interested
Write an invitation.	_____	_____	_____
Read more poetry.	_____	_____	_____
Learn lyrics to a romantic song.	_____	_____	_____
Call for information about movie schedules	_____	_____	_____
Other? _____	_____	_____	_____
_____	_____	_____	_____

12   Looking Back

Think about you have learned in this unit. Complete the form. Then tell the class your ideas.

A. The most useful thing I learned in this unit was _____
_____.

B. I would still like to learn _____.

C. I learned the most by working

_____ alone.   _____ with a partner.   _____ with a group.

D. The activity I liked best was   1   2   3   4   5   6   7   8   9   10   11

because _____.

E. The activity I liked least was   1   2   3   4   5   6   7   8   9   10   11

because _____.

INSTRUCTOR'S JOURNAL

_____

_____

_____

_____

_____

_____

Page 48	Correlates with:	Page 49
		Activity Masters: pages 31–34

AUTHORS' NOTES • • •

10 The three scenarios in this activity give learners practice in the higher-order thinking skill of problem solving. You can either have the entire class work on the same problem in small groups or you can have different groups work on different problems. If you choose the former, have the class read through all the situations and select the one they are most interested in. You may find that the small groups come up with different solutions to the problem. If different groups work on different problems, before they report their solutions to the class, make sure that everyone is familiar with each story. If your class is not familiar with problem solving, do the first story as a whole-group activity.

1. Learners read the story carefully.
2. Brainstorm with the class all the conflicts/problems within the story
3. Ask the class what advice they would give the different characters in the story.
4. After they give their advice, ask what they think would happen if the character followed the advice.
5. Have the class come to a consensus on the best solution to the problem.

11 "Options for Learning" offers additional work with poetry, song lyrics, using the telephone to get information, and writing invitations. Learners should choose an activity of interest and again we suggest that they work in pairs.

12 In "Looking Back" be sure you give students plenty of opportunity to reflect on their work and share their opinions about what they like and what they want to work on more.

FIELD TESTERS' NOTES • • •

12 *My students were most interested in reading more poetry and doing more exercises like in "Playing with the Story." They liked "Looking Back." They discovered they liked working in small teams of two or three, rather than working alone. They also enjoyed reading aloud which is something we do a lot in class.*

Linda Nachinoff
Brookline Adult and Community Education Program
Brookline, MA

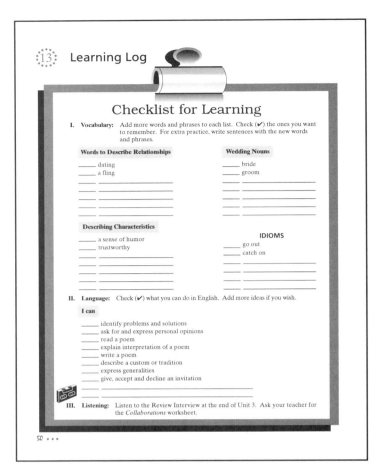

AUTHORS' NOTES • • •

The "Checklist for Learning" should be presented as in other units. See the *Assessment Program* for the mid-level self-assessment and course evaluation.

INSTRUCTOR'S JOURNAL

Page 50

Audiotape: Review Interview
Activity Masters: page 35
Workbook: page 38
Assessment Program

Correlates with:

50 • • •

Finding
Success in Corpus Christi, Texas

The first story in this unit comes from Corpus Christi, Texas. Corpus Christi is a port city on the Gulf of Mexico. The name of the city reflects the bicultural history of Texas. Although the first inhabitants of Texas were Native Americans, the first Europeans to explore the region were the Spanish in 1519. Texas was a part of Mexico until 1836. In Corpus Christi, many people work in chemical refineries, and many people still make a living from the sea. Many immigrants still come to Texas from Mexico and other parts of Latin America, but others come from all parts of the world seeking and finding success.

UNITED STATES (ALASKA)

CANADA

UNITED STATES

Texas

MEXICO

Maria Munoz's Story

A. Maria Munoz was born in San Diego, Texas. She has worked hard all of her life. When you read her story, notice her attitudes about work, learning, and life in general. Compare her experiences and her attitudes with your own.

B. As you read the story, think about what questions you would ask Maria if you could meet her.

Maria Munoz studies English in a computer lab and a class through the Corpus Christi Literacy Council. Maria would like to get her GED.

I started to work when I was about nine years old. My dad died, so we had to learn how to work. There were 12 brothers and sisters in our family and all of us went to work. It was an adventure.

We went to work near Fort Worth. The first job we had was picking cotton. It was very hard for us because, at first, we didn't know how to do it. We picked about 50 pounds of cotton at a time and it was too much for us to carry. It was kind of hard for me because I was small, but my mom and my family tried very hard. The job didn't pay a lot. It was less than 25 cents a pound. We had to get up at 5 o'clock in the morning to get to work. We got to work at about 8 o'clock in the morning, and we worked until 3 o'clock.

IDIOM
kind of

Mexico and Texas have argued about, modified, and shared a border for hundreds of years. In this long association, people on both sides of the border have also shared language, food, and music. The very popular "Conjunto" music uses accordion, 12-string guitar, bass, percussion, and other instruments.

I went to school a little, but my family had to take me out. I didn't have any shoes to go to school. I had to go out in the fields barefooted. Sometimes it was cold, and I didn't even have a coat. We went from place to place to work in the Rio Grande Valley. We worked in the cabbage, carrot, and potato fields. In the Valley we didn't have any school at all.

I wished I was able to go to school more, but at the same time, I was learning outside. I was learning things—like how much the boss was going to pay us. We had to work very hard, but it was for food to eat, so we had no choice.

I used to work in a tortilla factory in San Diego, Texas when I was eleven years old. I had to grind the corn, boil the corn, and make the tortillas. I also had to do all the cleaning. I earned a dollar from 5 o'clock in the morning until 8 o'clock at night. My boss, Mr. Marroquin, and his wife helped me, so we all worked together. They taught me how to run the business.

I was already married when my family and I went to Michigan. We worked in the cherries and strawberries in Coloma, near Grand Rapids. Each year we had to stay about two and a half months because we had to come back to Texas in September to register our kids for school. We had nine kids. They all worked except the baby who stayed back in Texas.

I am very proud. I learned how to work very young. I speak Spanish at home, but my daughters speak English, and my grandchildren speak English. I've been hard-working all my life, but it has been good because we had to learn through life how to live. Here I am, 62 years old—hard-working and earning only a little, but still alive.

In Maria's life, what ways have school and work been connected? How do you think Maria feels about her work life? Explain your idea.

PROVERB
English: Work and saving are the best lottery.
Spanish: El trabajo y la economía son la mejor lotería.

INSTRUCTOR'S JOURNAL

Page 52	Correlates with:	Page 53
Audiotape		Audiotape
Transparencies: page 11		Activity Masters: page 38
Workbook: page 17		Workbook: page 17

AUTHORS' NOTES ● ● ●

1   **A.–B.** Maria Munoz talks about her work life with dignity and grace. We feel that Maria's life is an example of a life well-lived and we hope that learners will be able to see similarities with their own struggles. For those learners who have come from comfortable economic backgrounds, we hope they will come to understand Maria's pride in her hard work and independent learning.

Before reading Maria's story, you can brainstorm initial opinions about work using *Transparencies* page 11 and the accompanying discussion questions. Learners can come up with ideas based on their own work, here and in their native countries, and on the work their parents or other family members do/did. We've found this is a fertile and complex topic for conversation. We've had classes where many of the learners were satisfied with their work life here, because they come from countries where there is little opportunity for education or profitable employment. However, we've also often encountered learners who were very dissatisfied with their jobs here because they were forced to accept "lower status" jobs than they had in their native countries. We think these issues should be discussed in class because sharing stories may help our learners to clarify their education and work goals

The "country box" gives information about "Conjunto" music. We think sharing music, like food, helps build the classroom community. Ask learners whether they know about this music and if they could bring some in. The Corpus Christi singer, Selena, (who died shortly before the interview with Maria Munoz and was one of the topics of the extended interview) sang an updated version of this kind of music. Learners could bring Selena's songs, or work songs from their native countries. Later in the unit, you will have a chance to review and extend this medium with "Sixteen Tons" by Merle Travis and "Living for the City" by Stevie Wonder.

FIELD TESTERS' NOTES ● ● ●

② Playing with Story Language

A. Maria Munoz is a **hard-working** and **proud** person. Even though she is over 60 years old, Maria is also very **active.** Reread the story and find words and phrases that demonstrate these characteristics.

hard-working _____

_____

proud _____

_____

active _____

_____

 B. Work with a partner to write a list of questions you would like to ask, if you could meet Maria.

_____

Reading Strategy	_____
Good readers connect their own experiences with what they read.	_____

_____

C. After you've finished your list, explain to others what questions you wanted to ask. Did you have similar questions?

		Indirect Questions
		I wondered **if** Maria likes computers. I asked **when** the class starts.
		In an indirect question, the noun clause begins with **if, whether (or not)**, or a **wh-question word**, the verb follows the noun, and a period ends the sentence.

D. Do you know an older person in your community? Ask some of the same questions you wanted to ask Maria. Share the answers with your class.

③ Doing It in English: Interviewing for Jobs

 A. Imagine you are the personnel manager of a successful and expanding computer store. Prepare a list of questions, direct or indirect, to ask the prospective employee.

OR

Imagine you are the prospective employee. Prepare a list of questions about job requirements, responsibilities, wages and benefits, and opportunities for advancement.

B. With a partner, roleplay a job interview. Take turns performing both parts. After you've practiced enough to feel comfortable, have a classmate or the teacher videotape the interview so you can see and hear your own language.

④ Journal Writing

In your journal, choose one of the following topics to write about:

1. Maria Munoz is an example of a hard-working, proud, and active older person. Write about a person you know who shows these same characteristics. Use specific examples to describe this person.

2. Maria considers herself a successful person. In what ways are you (or have you been) a successful person? Be specific.

PROVERB
English: Where the attempt is, there the success is, too.
Thai: ความพยายามอยู่ที่ไหน ความสำเร็จอยู่ที่นั่น

Learning Strategy
Knowledge is available everywhere, not just in school. Notice where and from whom you are learning, and start writing down what you learn in a notebook.

INSTRUCTOR'S JOURNAL

_____

_____

_____

_____

_____

_____

_____

Page 54 Workbook: pages 40–41, 48 Activity Masters: page 44	**Correlates with:**	**Page 55** Workbook: pages 42–45 Activity Masters: pages 39–40, 43–44

AUTHORS' NOTES • • •

2   **A.** This exercise gives learners the chance to go over the text closely and see how the adjectives fit in the context of the phrases and the story itself. Sharon McKay's upbeat advice on how to describe work skills (*Workbook,* page 40) is a natural adjunct to this activity. Groups could make lists of other descriptive words for Maria, for themselves, and for their partners. We like the proverb, *Knowledge is power,* (page 61), and we think that the more English vocabulary that learners acquire, the more power they have.

   B. At the intermediate level, we assume that a lot of informal peer correction and advice-giving goes on. Allow plenty of time for the partners to negotiate about the ways to ask questions.

   C. The concept of indirect questions is difficult for some learners. We know that many learners love grammar, but many bog down trying to understand all the rules theoretically. We think that it's more useful to practice and incorporate small bits of grammar in writing and speaking. Here, review the grammar in the box and use the illustration to show the relationship between the direct question on the list and the indirect question. With the whole group, you can elicit questions from the partners' lists and assist in the formation of indirect questions first. Then, learners can practice asking questions when they feel more comfortable with the structure. *Workbook* page 41 and *Activity Masters* page 44 offer more correlative practice with embedded questions.

3   **A.–B.** The first "Doing It in English" activity prepares learners for the extensive second activity. We think role-playing interviews are excellent ways to prepare for real-life interviews. Both parts of the activity will take several classes, but both individuals and the class benefit from intensive projects that result in a tangible product. When learners see or hear themselves, they can realistically assess their own skills.

FIELD TESTERS' NOTES • • •

2   **A.** *As a follow up to this activity, it would be great to have a story written by a former student or someone in the community. Then everyone could make up questions to ask and then compile them in a letter to the person, or invite the person to class to answer the students' questions.*

Andrea Parrella
The Adult Learning Program at English High
Jamaica Plain, MA

3   *Class was divided into three groups. Each group did one of the activities (A1, A2, and B). The activity was modified. Students were asked to apply the activity to their assigned reading. For example, for B they imagined how a character in a story would behave in an interview, given what they know or infer about that character. Each group then shared their collaborative effort with the remainder of the class, and the whole class discussed what was presented. Students unanimously agreed that they liked this activity because it "encouraged problem-solving."*

4   *Students were asked to write a three to five paragraph essay based upon the discussion of Activity 3. before writing, the . . . reading about Maria Munoz was discussed, with the writing assignment focusing on "success."*

Bobbie Lemontt
Suffolk University
Boston, MA

Other Voices from North America

UNITED STATES (ALASKA)

CANADA

UNITED STATES

Virginia

MEXICO

A. Look at the photographs of Cesar and Delilah. What do you think their jobs are? Explain.

B. When you read the following stories, compare your progress toward your own employment and education goals to Cesar's and Delilah's. Do you have a job now? How did you get it? Do you want to have the same job in five years?

Cesar Huamani lives in Fairfax County, Virginia.

Reading Strategy

Learn the specialized vocabulary of your job or hobby. Learn what the words mean, how to spell them, and how to pronounce them. Use the dictionary, a book on the subject, or ask an expert.

After I graduated from high school, I went to work in the American Embassy in Lima, Peru. I was in the Commercial Department, Library Section. Being in the library section, I was forced to study English and the computer. Years later, because of a bad economic situation in my country and my parents' concern about my sisters' welfare, they decided to leave the country. Because my father worked for the American Embassy for more than 20 years, he got resident visas for the whole family.

My father went first with my older sisters. Then my little sister wanted to go. She was 15 years old and she wouldn't be able to go unless somebody older was by her side. That older person was I. My mother asked me to go with my sister. "I don't want to go," I cried. But she was persistent. When I finally decided to go, she had already packed my things in a small suitcase days earlier. At first I didn't want to go, but I believed that deep in my heart I did want to go. I didn't realize that until years later, living here.

I started to work for a small landscaping company; I kind of liked it. Then two years later, my friend, who owned the company, offered to transfer the ownership of the company to me, and he showed me how to do that. Now I am the owner of C&C Landscaping Service.

IDIOMS
deep in my heart
kind of

Peru is the third largest country in South America. Almost 45 percent of its people are Native Americans. Many of these people, who speak Quechua or Aymara, are descendants of the Incas, who were conquered by Francisco Pizarro in the 1530s. In 1821 Peru declared its independence from Spain.

We do landscaping for commercial and residential areas. My crew and I go to different places in the Washington Metropolitan Area. We see different kinds of gardens and each one has its own way to show its beauty. When I saw the other guys doing the work with the plants and dirt, I wanted to do the work with them and not just work as the boss. I have learned to love the plants. I know about the bushes: azaleas, photinias, hollies. We plant bulbs, and I am getting to know more about the perennials like columbines and astilbe.*

I love to work with Mother Nature and what I like most is her beauty. This is why I am going to NOVA (Northern Virginia Community College) to study computer to design landscaped areas and then horticulture to know more about it. Later, I would like to transfer to the University of Maryland to complete my education for my own self-esteem. I've seen a lot of designs in the gardens I've worked in, and I feel that I can do that work very well.

IDIOM
Mother Nature

* These are names of plants. Look in your dictionary to learn how to pronounce them in English.

In 1995, Delilah Flores began teaching ESL in the Washington, D.C. Public Schools.

I completed my degree in Venezuela. I studied five years in the university to be a chemistry teacher. After that, I was working for three years at the high school level. I enjoyed working with teenagers, but after I worked with adults, at REEP (Arlington Education and Employment Program) I enjoyed that more.

My primary goal was to complete my Master's degree in biochemistry here.

I'm working as a clerk. I work with the microfilm. I develop the film, and then I retrieve the documents from the film I have already developed. I'm working for an insurance company. I've been there for about a year. It's very boring because you are doing the same thing all day long. Everything is production; you don't think, you just do it, that's it. It's not the way I have been brought up. I need to use my mind. That's why I am taking classes at night. I can't stop working, but I need to do something with my brain. I'm looking for a job as a medical technologist, working in a lab. I have done that job here, helping my sister as a volunteer and I have some experience that makes me feel confident enough to look for something in that field. I am also applying in Arlington Public Schools and Washington D.C. Public Schools to have the opportunity to teach.

Has having a good education from their native countries helped Cesar and Delilah here? In what ways?

Venezuela is a diverse country that includes a powerful petroleum industry, the urban capital of Caracas, and the Yanomami people of the Orinoco River Basin. The Orinoco River is the eighth longest river in the world. The Orinoco and the Amazon River form the largest river system in the world.

● ● ● 57

INSTRUCTOR'S JOURNAL

Page 56	**Correlates with:**	Page 57
Audiotape		**Audiotape**
Transparencies: page 12		**Workbook: pages 46–47**
Activity Masters: page 45		**Activity Masters: page 45**

AUTHORS' NOTES • • •

5   **A.** You may want to use the transparency of Cesar here (*Transparencies,* page 12) to begin the pre-reading discussion. Then, discuss the photo of Delilah in the text. Help learners to see whether or not the process of their "guessing" is based on what they can observe and logically infer. You could extend this activity by providing photos and asking small groups to observe and make guesses about the jobs. Making "educated" guesses is a practical strategy in all facets of life.

    B. These "Other Voices" stories encourage learners to read and compare with their own employment and education goals. Both Cesar and Delilah have clearly expressed goals, and we think this has helped them to be successful here.

    "More About Delilah Flores" on *Workbook* pages 46 and 47 continues the story of Delilah's success and shows a clear connection between learning English and job success.

FIELD TESTERS' NOTES • • •

Doing It in English: Talking About Goals

A. Both Cesar and Delilah have goals for themselves for school and work. They have short-term and long-term goals. Work with a partner to make a list of Cesar's and Delilah's goals. When you agree with each other, share your list with the class.

Learning Strategy

Dividing your goals into short-term and long-term goals helps you to remain realistic. Short-term goals are those you can accomplish in the near future. Long-term goals are your hopes and desires for your life.

B. Think about your own future. List your goals for work.

Short-term Goals	Long-term Goals
_____	_____
_____	_____
_____	_____
_____	_____

C. There are many ways to talk about goals:

I want to	I hope to
I'm going to	My plan is to
My idea is to	My goal is to
If I can, I will	My dream is to _____

D. Interview some of your classmates about their goals.

Name	What are your short-term goals?	What are your long-term goals?	What things can you do to reach your goals?

E. Looking at the answers to the chart questions, work with a small group to decide:

• Which goals seem most practical and realistic? Why do you think so?

• Do you think short-term goals should be more practical than long-term goals? Why or why not?

Together, write a paragraph that summarizes the group's conclusions. It's not necessary for each group member to agree. Read the paragraph to the rest of the class.

Learning Strategy

When you summarize an article or a conversation, you need to be objective. Personal opinions are not usually included in a summary.

PROVERB

English: To the stars through adversity.
Latin: Ad astra per aspera.

INSTRUCTOR'S JOURNAL

_____

_____

_____

_____

_____

_____

_____

_____

Page 58	Correlates with:	Page 59
Activity Masters: page 45		Actvity Masters: page 45

AUTHORS' NOTES • • •

6 **A.–B.** We've sometimes found it difficult to convince learners to set their goals at realistic levels. The process of going from Cesar and Delilah's goals to their own will help learners to naturally control the scope of their goals.

D. The questions on the grid are jumping off places for the class interviews. Challenge the class to come up with some more specific and complex questions such as:

- Have your long-term goals changed since you came here? (United States or Canada)
- Which is more important to do first: get a secure job or finish your education? Why?
- What problems do you face in reaching your goals?

E. Working in loosely-structured groups gives high-intermediate learners ample opportunity to communicate informally. The process of completing the activity may differ from group to group. That's fine, because it is authentic, complex communciation we are striving for, not parroted questions and answers. It's difficult to summarize conclusions and it's difficult to write a group paragraph. Here, again, it's in "doing it in English" that the learning occurs.

Because goal-setting is such an important process in our culture, you may want to ask learners to also write individually as Bobbie Lemontt did.

FIELD TESTERS' NOTES • • •

6 *Students worked in think/pair/share activity as directed in Activity A and then individually for Activity B. The activity was modified to include additional responses for both short and long-term goals: What methods or techniques would you use to achieve these goals. Students completed Activity D and E after attempting to cluster ideas and outlines. They were asked to write a four paragraph essay rather than merely a paragraph collaboratively. They were asked to restructure the body so that the format did NOT follow the boxes in the grid (short-term, long-term, "Things you can do") to follow a cause-effect format.*

Bobbie Lemontt
Suffolk University
Boston, MA

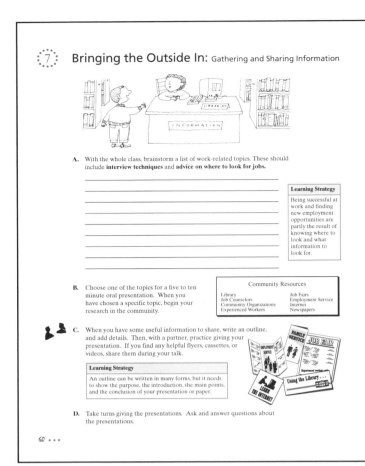

7 Bringing the Outside In: Gathering and Sharing Information

A. With the whole class, brainstorm a list of work-related topics. These should include **interview techniques** and **advice on where to look for jobs.**

_____
_____
_____
_____
_____
_____
_____
_____

> **Learning Strategy**
> Being successful at work and finding new employment opportunities are partly the result of knowing where to look and what information to look for.

B. Choose one of the topics for a five to ten minute oral presentation. When you have chosen a specific topic, begin your research in the community.

> **Community Resources**
> Library
> Job Counselors
> Community Organizations
> Experienced Workers
> Job Fairs
> Employment Service
> Internet
> Newspapers

C. When you have some useful information to share, write an outline, and add details. Then, with a partner, practice giving your presentation. If you find any helpful flyers, cassettes, or videos, share them during your talk.

> **Learning Strategy**
> An outline can be written in many forms, but it needs to show the purpose, the introduction, the main points, and the conclusion of your presentation or paper.

D. Take turns giving the presentations. Ask and answer questions about the presentations.

8 Ideas for Action: Sharing for Power

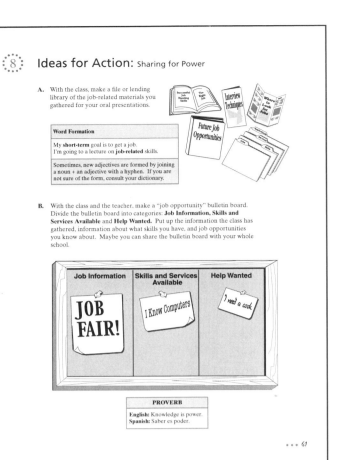

A. With the class, make a file or lending library of the job-related materials you gathered for your oral presentations.

> **Word Formation**
> My **short-term** goal is to get a job. I'm going to a lecture on **job-related** skills.
>
> Sometimes, new adjectives are formed by joining a noun + an adjective with a hyphen. If you are not sure of the form, consult your dictionary.

B. With the class and the teacher, make a "job opportunity" bulletin board. Divide the bulletin board into categories: **Job Information, Skills and Services Available** and **Help Wanted.** Put up the information the class has gathered, information about what skills you have, and job opportunities you know about. Maybe you can share the bulletin board with your whole school.

Job Information	Skills and Services Available	Help Wanted
JOB FAIR!	I Know Computers	I need a cook.

> **PROVERB**
> **English:** Knowledge is power.
> **Spanish:** Saber es poder.

INSTRUCTOR'S JOURNAL

_____
_____
_____
_____
_____
_____
_____

Page 60	Correlates with:	Page 61
Activity Masters: page 41		**Activity Masters: page 41, 46**

AUTHORS' NOTES • • •

7 The information-gathering and sharing techniques practiced in these "Bringing the Outside In" activities are useful for many topics. Many communities have librarians who are glad to give library tours and demonstrations (of the catalogue system, Internet, etc).

A. Learners will easily be able to come up with the list of work-related topics. In the class conversation, try to help learners narrow topics as much as possible.

B.–D. We strongly endorse oral presentations as a holistic way to use and extend all English skills. In the research phase, learners need to read, ask questions, listen for comprehension, and write notes. In the presentation phase, learners need to review and use proper grammar, syntax, and vocabulary. Learners need to organize material and the presentation itself. They need to work on pronunciation and speaking (with a partner, teacher, or volunteer). Finally, leaners need to try to understand their audience, ask learners questions to check for listener comprehension, and perform in a real-life situation. Beyond this, learners should evaluate their own presentations, learn to accept evaluation from peers, and listen to, understand, and evaluate others.

8 **A.–B.** "Ideas for Action" is a logical extension of Activity 7. Making a class or school resource center compounds the knowledge and makes it easily accessible to all. We have seen learners become energized over such activities where the real-life usefulness is evident. Some learners will already be familiar with libraries, presentations, and creating and sharing of materials, but, for some, these will be new and empowering experiences. Help only as much as learners seem to need you. The more independently they can work, the more easily they can translate such activities into other sectors of their lives.

FIELD TESTERS' NOTES • • •

Other Voices: The Poetry, Prose, and Music of Work

A. Because work is one of the basic elements of life, many varieties of writing reflect ideas and feelings about work. While you read the American examples below, compare the ideas and emotions expressed with those of your native language.

B. Although some words may be unfamiliar, see how much you can understand from context alone.

1

Early to bed, early to rise
makes a man
healthy, wealthy, and wise.
Benjamin Franklin

2

All work and no play
makes Jack a dull boy.
Nursery Rhyme

3

A MAN WORKS
FROM SUN TO SUN
BUT A WOMAN'S WORK
IS NEVER DONE
An old saying

4

His father works some days for fourteen hours
And you can bet he barely makes a dollar
His mother goes to scrub the floors for many
And you'd best believe she barely makes a penny
Living just enough, just enough for the city . . .
from the song:
"Living for the City"
Stevie Wonder

5

Now some people say a man's made out of mud,
But a poor man's made out of muscle and blood,
Muscle and blood, skin and bones,
A mind that's weak and a back that's strong.

CHORUS:
You load sixteen tons and what do you get
Another day older and deeper in debt,
Saint Peter, don't you call me 'cause I can't go,
I owe my soul to the company store.
from the song:
"Sixteen Tons"
by Merle Travis

6

The Ant and the Grasshopper—Once upon a time there were two insects who were friends: an ant and a grasshopper. It was summertime and the weather was warm, sunny, and pleasant. The ant worked hard. He carried food into his home all day long. The grasshopper said, "Why don't you quit working so hard and relax with me? It's a beautiful day and we can just eat when we are hungry." The ant refused. He said, "I must prepare for the winter when the weather will be cold and we can't go outside to gather food." So the ant worked, and the grasshopper played. When winter came, the ant was comfortable in his cozy nest and his stomach was full. The grasshopper knocked on his door and begged to come in. The ant was kind, so he let his friend share his home and food. But he scolded his friend. He said, "You are lazy and irresponsible. You should have worked and prepared for hard times. Now, you know better." **From Aesop's Fables**

IDIOM
know better

Reading Strategy
When you read a poem, a song, or a fable, look for the "moral" or lesson you are supposed to learn.

What lesson did you learn from this story?
Do you know this story or one like it?
Who told you the story?

INSTRUCTOR'S JOURNAL

Page 62
Activity Masters: page 42

Correlates with:

Page 63
Activity Masters: page 42

62 ● ● ●

AUTHORS' NOTES ● ● ●

9   **A.–B.** In this "Other Voices" activity, we again ask learners to search for more than the surface meaning of words. We want learners to understand emotions and cultural ideas as whole pieces, not as overly precise sentence by sentence translations. We've used mostly traditional work sayings here. Learners may want to compare them not only with their native language sayings, but with more current American voices such as expressed in rap or alternative music.

You can use this activity as a catalyst for reading or telling folktales or listening to music lyrics. We've known many learners who listen to American music not only for pleasure but also to understand current, nonstandard English. With the class, brainstorm a list of radio stations, formats (top 40, talk radio, etc), and programs. Ask learners to listen to a specific radio show about a current topic. Tape it and debrief with learners the next day. This is a time-consuming activity. However, it gives real-life importance to the listening, and also gives you a chance to do an informal assessment of learners' listening comprehension.

FIELD TESTERS' NOTES ● ● ●

9   *I used this activity for small group discussion (three in a group)—"Ice Breaker" to encourage students to get to know each other . . . Students were asked to come up with some similar sayings to create "bumper stickers." It would be useful to leave a line for students to formulate the thesis, theme, or control idea in their own words for each example.*

Bobbie Lemontt
Suffolk University
Boston, MA

10 Sharing Ideas: Mood, Rhythm, and Meaning

A. Choose one of the readings to study closely. Read the passage. Read it, again, out loud to yourself, a partner, or your teacher.

B. Now, answer the questions about the passage you studied. There might be more than one correct way to answer each question. Try to answer in complete sentences.

What is the **mood** of the passage? Is it happy, sad, bitter, or philosophical?

_____

_____

What words or word patterns give you clues to the meaning of the text?

_____

_____

> **Reading Strategy**
> You can understand the emotions, or **mood,** expressed in a piece of literature by analyzing such things as topic, vocabulary, rhythm, and repetition.

Can you identify a pattern or rhythm in the words or sentence patterns? What elements make the pattern?

C. Talk to a student who read the same text as you did. Does he/she agree with your answers?

D. Choose your favorite text and paraphrase it. Read your words to the class.

_____

_____

_____

_____

_____

_____

11 Learning About Each Other: Cultural Sayings About Work

A. Do you and your classmates share some of the same feelings about work as each other and the texts? Think about some expressive idioms, poems, stories or songs from your native language that comment about work. Write it in your native language, then write it in English.

B. Ask a partner to help you to edit your English writing to make it clear and correct.

> **Learning Strategy**
> When you edit, don't forget to check the basics: spelling, capitalization, punctuation, pronoun reference, and subject-verb agreement.

C. With the whole class, decide how to produce the writing: in a book, on a bulletin board, or sharing a performance at your local community center.

INSTRUCTOR'S JOURNAL

_____

_____

_____

_____

_____

_____

_____

Page 64	Correlates with:	Page 65
		Workbook: page 49

AUTHORS' NOTES ● ● ●

10 As you ask your class to critically study the readings (pages 62 and 63), you may find that they know a lot about "mood, rhythm, and meaning" that translates from their own languages and experiences into English. We think that by sharing your ideas, you can expand learners' literary vocabularies and also give a boost to those who need to take the GED or to eventually take freshman English in college.

A. We've heard many theories about whether or not it is proper to ask ESL learners to read out loud. We think it's good practice and that learners will enjoy sharing with a partner. However, don't press reticent learners; they can practice as much as they wish at home.

B. Before you begin this activity, reinforce the idea that there may be more than one correct way to answer each question. You may also want to mention that not every answer will be correct. Only those answers whose direct relationship to the language of the text are clearly delineated can be "in the ballpark."

11 A. Some members of the class may feel more comfortable with an English idiom, poem, story, or song. Some of the younger people in your class may have been here long enough to identify with our "youth" culture more than the native culture of their parents' generation.

B. Some learners find it challenging to edit and be edited by their peers. They are unsure of what to look for and what to correct. If learners begin by editing basics, especially spelling, capitalization, and end punctuation, the exercise will not seem overly daunting. Later, learners can concentrate on subject/verb agreement, pronoun reference, or particular structures you've worked on in class.

C. Andrea Parrella suggests expanding the "Learning About Each Other" to include families and children in the community.

FIELD TESTERS' NOTES ● ● ●

11 *Students can compile a list of sayings about work they could translate from their native languages. Each student could choose one that he or she feels strongly about and paint or decoupage a box or journal or folder cover with the saying in fancy lettering and decorate it as a reminder of their own values or as a gift for their children, or family, or friends. Students could share fables about work from their own cultures—maybe turn it into a children's book with illustrations. Then, they can find an audience: children they know or a local elementary class.*

Andrea Parrella
The Adult Learning Program at English High
Jamaica Plain, MA

12 Think It Over: Varieties of English

A. In Maria's, Cesar's, and Delilah's stories, each has a slightly different style. In the other readings, the style, vocabulary, and grammar are much different. Work in a small group to discuss opinions about English. Use some of the following statements to get you started:

Learning Strategy

Find friends who speak different varieties of English. Ask for help understanding pronunciation and idioms that differ from standard English.

Standard English is the only correct English.

American English is not as formal as British English.

You can't learn to speak English well if you practice with immigrants and other people with accents or dialects.

There is no reason to learn "street" English.

It's no good to read English literature that contains slang.

A person can't learn a language well without knowing all the grammar.

To get a great job, a person can't have a strong accent.

B. After talking with your group, ask your teacher to put up three signs around the classroom: **AGREE, DISAGREE,** and **UNSURE.** When a classmate or the teacher reads each statement, stand near the sign that expresses your opinion. Write the results on the board.

C. For the bulletin board, compile a list of what the majority of the class agrees about regarding the English language. Also, leave room on the bulletin board for alternative opinions that the class discussed.

IDIOM
leave room

Agreeing, Disagreeing, and Being Unsure

Agree:	Disagree:	Unsure:
I agree with you (or with that idea).	I don't agree.	I can't decide.
I think that's true.	I'm not sure I can agree with that idea.	I'm just not sure.
I think that's right.	I can't agree with that completely.	I think I need some more time to think about this issue.
You've expressed my idea perfectly.	I'm afraid we are not in agreement.	

13 Options for Learning: Finding Employment Success

A. How do you want to be able to use English to help in employment? Check (✔) your answers. Add other ideas if you wish.

	Already Do	Want to Learn	Not Interested
Speak well and be confident in an interview.	_____	_____	_____
Ask complex questions on the job or applying for a job.	_____	_____	_____
Explain short-term and long-term goals.	_____	_____	_____
Find employment information in your community.	_____	_____	_____
Other? _____	_____	_____	_____

14 Looking Back

Think about your learning. Complete this form. Then tell the class your ideas.

A. The most useful thing I learned in this unit was _____

_____

B. I would still like to learn _____.

C. I learned the most by working

_____ alone. _____ with a partner. _____ with a group.

D. The activity I liked best was 1 2 3 4 5 6 7 8 9 10 11 12 13

because _____

E. The activity I liked least was 1 2 3 4 5 6 7 8 9 10 11 12 13

because _____

INSTRUCTOR'S JOURNAL

_____

_____

_____

_____

_____

_____

_____

_____

Page 66
Workbook: page 50
Activity Masters: page 42

Correlates with:

Page 67
Activity Masters: pages 43–46

66 ● ● ●

AUTHORS' NOTES ● ● ●

12 **A.–B.** Learners have widely differing beliefs about language learning. Talking about varieties of English provides learners with a venue to express their own, often strongly held, views. At the same time, the topic also gives them the opportunity to work on the complex register of language for agreeing, disagreeing, and being unsure.

Rarely have we had classes where learners didn't become comfortable enough with each other to debate serious issues. By this time, you will know your class well enough to know whether this activity will work with your group. The statements could also be used as a starting point for a writing assignment.

13 Even if learners are not currently concerned about employment, assure them that the underlying communicative and life-skill tasks are useful in other sectors of their lives as well. Please refer to *Activity Masters* pages 43–46 for the appropriate activity sheets.

14 For C. of "Looking Back," try expanding the answer to include the learner's opinion of why he or she learned most by working alone, with a partner, or with a group. The answer itself is not important, but we want to continue encouraging learners to reflect on their own learning.

FIELD TESTERS' NOTES ● ● ●

14 *Students completed the evaluation form individually then tallied the responses. The class was divided into two groups, with each side taking an opposing viewpoint (Point/Counterpoint) about the most popular answer. For example, one group of students was asked to defend the advantages of working alone. They were asked to provide specific examples from the actvities to support their position.*

Bobbie Lemontt
Suffolk University
Boston, MA

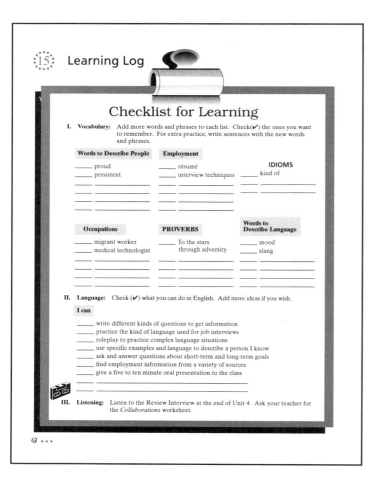

Checklist for Learning

I. Vocabulary: Add more words and phrases to each list. Check(✔) the ones you want to remember. For extra practice, write sentences with the new words and phrases.

Words to Describe People
_____ proud
_____ persistent
_____ _____
_____ _____
_____ _____

Employment
_____ résumé
_____ interview techniques
_____ _____
_____ _____
_____ _____

IDIOMS
_____ kind of
_____ _____
_____ _____

Occupations
_____ migrant worker
_____ medical technologist
_____ _____
_____ _____
_____ _____

PROVERBS
_____ To the stars through adversity
_____ _____
_____ _____

Words to Describe Language
_____ mood
_____ slang
_____ _____
_____ _____
_____ _____

II. Language: Check (✔) what you can do in English. Add more ideas if you wish.

I can
_____ write different kinds of questions to get information
_____ practice the kind of language used for job interviews
_____ roleplay to practice complex language situations
_____ use specific examples and language to describe a person I know
_____ ask and answer questions about short-term and long-term goals
_____ find employment information from a variety of sources
_____ give a five to ten minute oral presentation to the class
_____ _____
_____ _____

III. Listening: Listen to the Review Interview at the end of Unit 4. Ask your teacher for the *Collaborations* worksheet.

68 • • •

AUTHORS' NOTES • • •

15 Learners can initially work with the Review Interview as a class, but some may want to listen several times individually or in a small group. If you get the chance, tape your own interviews and bring them in for the whole class, especially for those who are unsure of their listening skills.

Have your class discuss the learning log (along with *Workbook* and *Activity Masters* assessment) as Bobbie Lemontt's class did. Take the learners' suggestions to modify the materials to suit their needs.

FIELD TESTERS' NOTES • • •

Students discussed the idea of using a Learning Log and the ways it helps/hinders learning.

Bobbie Lemontt
Suffolk University
Boston, MA

INSTRUCTOR'S JOURNAL

Page 68	Correlates with:
Audiotape	
Workbook: pages 51–52	
Activity Masters: page 47	
Assessment Program	

Unit 5

Special Communities
Refugees in Comer and Atlanta, Georgia

The stories in this unit are from Comer, Georgia and Atlanta, Georgia. Comer is a small town 75 miles east of Atlanta. It is the home of Jubilee Partners, a Christian community dedicated to helping others and living simply. Jubilee established a Refugee Welcome Center in 1979. Refugees stay for two to three months, study English, and learn about life in the United States. Since 1979, almost 2,000 refugees have come to Jubilee. During this time more than 300 volunteers from all over the world have worked there teaching, doing construction, gardening and maintenance work. Many of the refugees resettle in the Atlanta area.

Georgia

Stories from Jubilee: Enver Softic and Senita Roje

A. Discuss these questions with your class: What is a refugee? What is a volunteer? How much did you know about the United States before you came here? Did your expectations differ from reality?

B. Read the stories. Compare your early experiences in the United States to the writers' experiences.

Enver Softic, his wife Samka and daughter Elvedina are from Bosnia. They came to Jubilee before settling in Atlanta where Enver's brother is already living.

We have been here seventeen days. Jubilee people and my relatives, who are already living in Atlanta, met us at the airport. We didn't expect my relatives to be there. We arrived at Jubilee at 1 A.M. and we were surprised that people stayed up to meet us. At night we couldn't see anything but in the morning we woke up and looked around. It was so peaceful and natural.

We feel comfortable at Jubilee. The partners* and volunteers here are good people. They take us everywhere and they help prepare us for our life in Atlanta. We visit places, play soccer, and go fishing. We don't have the city crowd here and we don't worry about anything. We study English, but it is very hard for me and my wife because we are older. I know a little German, but I think I will learn English slowly.

We don't know much about Atlanta yet, but anything will be better than before. Before the war, our community in Bosnia was super. We could go everywhere and not be afraid of guns. We could sleep out in the yard. We could open our house to our friends.

> Why does Enver feel comfortable at Jubilee?
> Would you feel comfortable in a place like Jubilee?

*Partners are the people who are permanent members of the community. They live and work at Jubilee year round.

I have been in the United States for only one month and I came right to Jubilee. Many people have information about the United States in Bosnia through television, movies, newspapers and books. I thought I knew everything, but I didn't know what awaited. I did not expect to be living in a rural place like Jubilee. I expected to be living in an apartment in Atlanta right away.

Jubilee is different. My first day here I saw trees and animals and I felt the fresh air and the quiet. Sometimes I think time has stopped here. My people have a very strong pain. Sometimes it is difficult for us but the people here help us by being so nice. Also, here life is easy. Here I can take long walks and think. I have so many things to think about. I can talk with people and I can relax.

I study English here but I think I learn most of my English after class when we socialize and just talk to the volunteers.

Yesterday I visited Atlanta and saw many of my people. I think I am prepared to go now. I don't know about my future. What I want and what I must do are two different things. I must speak better English. I must work. I *must stop dreaming. I *have* stopped dreaming. Slowly I stopped because reality is different from my dreams.

I would like to live like I did in Europe before the war. I needed only a few months more to finish college. I would like to teach Bosnian children or American children. Children are children. I would like this so much. I want to find a job in Atlanta that fits my personality. Something where I am with many people, like in a boutique.

Senita Roje is from Bosnia. She is living and studying English at Jubilee. She plans to settle in Atlanta.

> How did Jubilee help Senita?
> How is your arrival similar to or different from these stories?

C. Summarize the stories in your own words.

Reading Strategy

To summarize, find the main idea and details that are necessary to understand the story. A summary is objective and does not include the reader's reactions.

INSTRUCTOR'S JOURNAL

Page 70

Audiotape: Story on tape
Transparency: page 14

Correlates with:

Page 71

Audiotape: Story on tape

AUTHORS' NOTES • • •

The stories in this unit center around the arrival of refugees into the United States. They begin their life at a unique community in northeast Georgia. Jubilee Partners has been helping refugees' transition into American society since 1980. It is a community founded on the principles of the Christian faith and its mission is to help the oppressed. Refugees of all faiths and nationalities are equally welcome and their beliefs are respected and valued, be they Christians, Buddhists, Moslems, or other.

The second theme of the chapter focuses on volunteers. Stories of immigrants and citizens describe the hows and whys of community volunteer work.

To introduce these themes you might want to discuss what the refugee status means and what a volunteer does. Some students may not know what makes one person a refugee and another a different type of immigrant. Many immigrants may have stories of fear, oppression, and grief similar to a Bosnian or Vietnamese refugee. However, refugee status is a political decision. Also, discuss types of volunteer work people do in their countries to link the theme to their own lives.

1 With the overhead transparency, discuss the differences between the two environments. Ask the class which picture best depicts their idea of the United States before they arrived. Have learners read the stories and discuss the questions in the box.

After the initial reading you may want half the class to summarize Enver's (pronounced En veer) story and the other half to summarize Senita's (pronounced sen EE tah) story. They can then pair off and share their summaries with each other.

If your students are not familiar with giving summaries, we suggest you choose one of the stories to work on with the whole class. Ask learners to tell you what the story is about. Write their ideas, exactly as they state them, on the board. Next, ask the class to look at the sentences on the board and find the ones that refer to small details. Erase those sentences as they find them. Now ask them to find the sentences that tell the main idea. Circle those sentences. Together compose a summary from the phrases and sentences circled on the board.

FIELD TESTERS' NOTES • • •

1 *The summary was the most difficult part for students, but it was also the one chosen as most helpful. Most of the students had never written a summary before in English. The summary was assigned as homework. The next day, we put on the board the ideas we agreed were necessary for a summary. Then students in groups of four compared their summaries. Some students found the group-sharing most helpful, others found it the least helpful. I followed up the group work with a mini-lesson on plagiarism and proper use of quotation marks.*

Gayle Roby
Bunker Hill Community College
Charlestown, MA

2 Playing with Story Language

> Who, **what**, **where**, **when**, **why**, and **how** questions ask for information.
> They ask for details in a reading.
> For example: **Where** is Enver from? Enver is from **Bosnia.**
> Bosnia is a detail from the story.

A. Write five information questions for each story.

Enver Softic's Story

1. _____
2. _____
3. _____
4. _____
5. _____

Senita Roje's Story

1. _____
2. _____
3. _____
4. _____
5. _____

B. Ask a partner to answer your questions. Check your partner's answers.

> Bosnia and Herzegovina was part of the former Republic of Yugoslavia. Since the spring of 1992, the country has been involved in civil strife among different ethnic groups. Many people have died and family members have been separated from each other. The international community has been trying to find a peaceful solution to the conflict.

3 Learning About Each Other: Our Lives Here

A. Work with a small group and find out about each other's first few months in the United States.

Name	Who helped you the most? How?	How did you learn about American culture?	How did you find out about English classes?

Senita Roje says that what she wants to do and what she must do are two different things.

B. List things that you *want* to do and things that you *must* do.

Want	Must
_____	_____
_____	_____
_____	_____

Expressing Obligation and Desire

Obligation	Desire
I must cook dinner now.	**I want to** eat at a restaurant.
I have to cook dinner now.	**I would like to** eat at a restaurant.

Must and **have to** are used to express obligation.
Want to and **would like to** express desire.

INSTRUCTOR'S JOURNAL

_____

_____

_____

_____

_____

_____

_____

Page 72	Correlates with:	Page 73
Workbook: pages 54–55		**Workbook: page 56**
Activity Masters: page 50		**Activity Masters: pages 51–52**

AUTHORS' NOTES • • •

2 As a way for learners to focus on the facts of the story and as an aid to remembering information, students write questions about the stories. You may want to review the formation of wh- questions and remind them that they should be able to answer their own questions. They will be checking the work of their partners. In the *Workbook,* students will learn more about Jubilee and have additional work in making up questions.

As an additional activity, you may want to first pair students with an editing partner. After learners write their questions, they should show them to their "editor" to check the structure of the questions. This partner does not answer the questions. When learners are happy with their questions, they pair off with a new partner to answer each other's questions.

3 In "Learning About Each Other" activities, learners share information about their own experiences of their early days in a new country. Here and in the *Activity Masters,* learners have an opportunity to communicate in a natural, relaxed way, concentrating on communication and not on structure.

In the second activity, learners review the functions for expressing obligation and desire. The box at the bottom of the page gives examples of forms and functions. Learners can use the language found in the story and reflect on their own desires and obligations.

As an extended activity, you can have learners share their lists with a small group of classmates.

FIELD TESTERS' NOTES • • •

2 *Writing information questions required a review of question forms such as do, does, etc., and a few examples, but it served as a good grammar review once they got going.*

Marge Matoba
Fremont Adult School
Sacramento, CA

3 *The students discussed a lot of Senita's ideas about having to stop dreaming and the role of dreams in relation to reality. It was a great discussion.*

Marge Matoba
Fremont Adult School
Sacramento, CA

4 Journal Writing

In your journal write about **one** of the following:

1. Has life in the United States been what you expected it to be?

2. Think about someone who helped you when you first arrived. Who was this person? How did he/she help you?

5 Doing It in English: Asking for Help

A. Read the conversations. Practice different ways to request help and respond to requests for help.

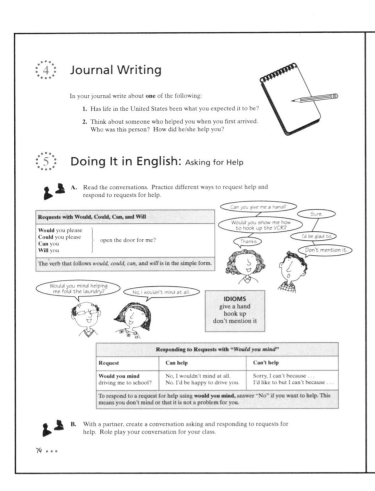

Requests with Would, Could, Can, and Will	
Would you please **Could** you please **Can** you **Will** you	open the door for me?

The verb that follows *would, could, can,* and *will* is in the simple form.

IDIOMS
give a hand
hook up
don't mention it

Responding to Requests with *"Would you mind"*		
Request	**Can help**	**Can't help**
Would you mind driving me to school?	No, I wouldn't mind at all. No, I'd be happy to drive you.	Sorry, I can't because . . . I'd like to but I can't because . . .

To respond to a request for help using **would you mind,** answer "No" if you want to help. This means you don't mind or that it is not a problem for you.

B. With a partner, create a conversation asking and responding to requests for help. Role play your conversation for your class.

74 • • •

6 Think It Over: Reading Graphs and Tables

A. Graphs and tables give you information in a short, clear visual way. The following graph and table give information about immigration in the United States.

Reading Strategy

Bar graphs can be used to show quantities. You must read two scales: the **horizontal →** scale and the **vertical ↑ scale.** These scales are labeled to tell you what the graph is measuring.

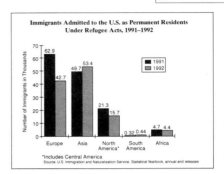

Immigrants Admitted to the U.S. as Permanent Residents Under Refugee Acts, 1991–1992

*Includes Central America
Source: U.S. Immigration and Naturalization Service, Statistical Yearbook, annual and releases

B. Read the bar graph to answer the questions. Check your answer with your partner.

1. What is the topic of the graph? _____

2. What does the vertical scale measure? _____

3. Was there an increase or a decrease in the number of refugees admitted to the United States in 1992? _____

4. Where did most of the refugees come from in 1991 and 1992? _____

5. Which continent had an increase of refugees admitted to the United States in 1992? _____

• • • 75

INSTRUCTOR'S JOURNAL

_____

_____

_____

_____

_____

_____

_____

Page 74 Workbook: pages 57–60	Correlates with:	Page 75

AUTHORS' NOTES ● ● ●

4 If students have trouble organizing their thoughts, remind them that they can use a web diagram to brainstorm ideas before they write. As in all other units, learners should feel free to write about other topics related to the unit. You may want to brainstorm possible subjects with the class.

5 The functions in this unit of asking for and offering help, relate to the themes of the unit. The refugees needed help and volunteers offered help in many ways. There are a variety of ways to present the functions. The boxes offer explanations of the use of modals to make polite requests. The two sample dialogues put the functions in a context.

Students often get confused when trying to answer a question that begins with "would you mind." You can do a whole-group activity to practice this structure. One student thinks of a request and calls on a classmate to do something. *"Would you mind opening the door?"* The classmate listens and responds. If he says *"No, I wouldn't mind,"* he would get up and open the door.

Role plays are an excellent way to practice the functions in a variety of contexts. An extension of Part B would be to create a number of different situations where learners would need to ask for or respond to requests for help. Give students a brief time (three to five minutes) to prepare the role play for the class. The key here is not to write out the conversation, but to spontaneously improvise a situation.

In the *Workbook,* learners concentrate on life-skill competencies that often confuse new arrivals as they did Nermina Silnovic. Learners can practice asking for help with the forms or getting information in the context of health and banking.

6 Additional questions relating to the bar graph could be:

- What happened in 1992 that would cause an increase in the Asian refugee population?
- What questions does the information in this graph raise in your mind?
- How would you find the answers to your questions?

FIELD TESTERS' NOTES ● ● ●

6 *The bar graph was assigned as homework. We had recently read a bar graph in our current text, so this was review. Several students found this exercise the least useful, but for a small number it was the most helpful and most enjoyable. I used Question 4 to clarify the difference between "most of the" and "the most."*

Gayle Roby
Bunker Hill Community College
Charlestown, MA

An opinion poll is a survey of what people think about a topic. A small part of the population answers questions and this information gives us an idea of what the general population may be thinking. Gallup is one company that gets information about public opinion. In 1993 the Gallup Poll survey asked the following question:

"How important—very important or not important—do you think each of the following factors should be in determining whether or not people from other countries should be admitted to live in the United States?"

The table shows the results of the poll.

Reading Strategy

Look at the **title** and the **headings** of each category to learn what kind of information is given in the table.

Factors for Admission to the United States—Gallup Poll 7/93 to 11/93			
FACTORS	*Very important*	*Not important*	*No opinion*
They should have occupational skills.	78%	21%	1%
They should have relatives who are American citizens.	56%	42%	2%
They are facing religious persecution.	65%	32%	3%
They are suffering from economic hardship.	47%	49%	4%
They have money to invest in business in the United States.	50%	48%	2%
They are facing political persecution.	64%	31%	5%

 C. Look at the table and discuss these questions in a small group.

1. What is the topic of this table?

2. What did the people interviewed think was the most important factor? Why do you think this was the most important one?

3. What did the people interviewed think was the least important factor? Why do you think this one was not as important?

4. Which factor do you think is most important?

 (7) **Other Voices from North America:** Being a Volunteer

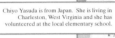 **A.** Work in a group with other students. Read **one** of the following stories. Practice retelling the story in your own words with your partners. Be sure to retell the important points. *Remember, you are the experts for this story.* When everyone is ready, change groups. Form new groups of four people with one person from each of the original groups. Tell them about the story you read. Listen to them tell you about the stories they read.

Vlasta Zhang (third from the left) is from Croatia and has lived in the United States for four years. She has been a volunteer at Jubilee Partners for two years. She was a chemist in her country.

1. When I arrived in the United States, I came as a tourist. I came to visit friends. It was my choice to visit the United States, but the Bosnian refugees who came here had no choice. They *had* to change where they lived. I volunteer as a translator because the Croatian and Bosnian languages are very similar.

I always try to put myself in the refugees' position. I ask myself what I would need and want if I were in the same situation. Much of my work is just listening. When they are sad, I cry with them. When they are happy, I laugh with them. After they move to Atlanta, they call me up to tell me all about their new lives. They say, "Vlasta, guess what? I got a new car!" or "Vlasta, guess what? I got a new hair cut!" They call and tell me when their children do well in school. We remain friends.

Chiyo Yasuda is from Japan. She is living in Charleston, West Virginia and she has volunteered at the local elementary school.

2. The first year I was in Charleston, I volunteered as an exchange teacher. I taught Kindergarten through sixth grade. I had fifteen classes and I taught each class for 45 minutes, once a week. I taught them about Japan and the Japanese language. I was so impressed because the children were so smart and so sweet. I was scared at first that maybe they wouldn't like a Japanese person but I never felt prejudice from them. None of them were mean to me. I had a good experience.

INSTRUCTOR'S JOURNAL

Page 76	Correlates with:	Page 77
Workbook: page 61		Transparency: page 15

AUTHORS' NOTES • • •

6 As an extension to Part C, take a poll of your students and determine what they consider to be the important factors for admission to the United States. You can also have them consider what the important factors would be for admission to their countries. Determine the percentage of the class that rated each factor *very important, not important,* or *no opinion.*

7 This jigsaw reading is meant to enhance the learners' skills of summarizing and paraphrasing that were introduced in previous units.

When doing a jigsaw reading, the whole class is divided into groups of four people. In the first group, "the reading group," learners read the story and practice retelling it in their own words to each other. It is very important that the group understand that they are to read only one of the stories. When all the students in each group are ready, they move to their second group, "the sharing group."

FIRST GROUP		SECOND GROUP	
A	A	A	B
A	A	C	D
B	B	A	B
B	B	C	D
C	C	A	B
C	C	C	D
D	D	A	B
D	D	C	D

In this group, they retell their stories to each other. Remind them that it is very important that they listen carefully to each other so that they understand the new information. They should be encouraged to ask each other questions and take notes if they like.

FIELD TESTERS' NOTES • • •

7 *I did the jigsaw reading in more detail and more controlled than suggested. I wrote comprehension questions such as:*

Vlasta Zhang
- *Where is she from?*
- *How long has she lived in the United States?*
- *Describe how she works.*
- *How is she different from the Bosnian refugees?*

Chiyo Yasuda
- *Where is she from?*
- *Where does she live now?*
- *What kind of volunteer work has she done?*
- *Describe her volunteer experience.*

Steve Barrigar
- *What kind of job does he have?*
- *What two organizations does he do volunteer work for?*
- *How does he find time to do volunteer work?*

Marcos Almanza
- *What organizations does he volunteer for?*
- *How does Desarrollo Comunal raise money?*
- *What kinds of things do they do with the money they have?*
- *Why does he like to do volunteer work?*

Marge Matoba
Fremont Adult School
Sacramento, CA

3. I volunteer with the American Red Cross. The first project I worked on was putting together school kits for Somali children living in refugee camps. Also, I'm vice-president of the Friends of Togo organization. This group was set up by Peace Corps volunteers who used to work in Togo. We give aid to Togo for small development projects. I volunteer to help people out. I've had an interest in working with international organizations for a long time. It's something I enjoy. People ask me how I find the time. I just say that if it's important for you to do something, then you will do it. It means being organized and scheduling things, but I just make sure I set aside the time for my volunteer work.

Steve Barrigar is from the United States. He is a computer specialist in Washington, D.C. He is studying for his Master's Degree in International Transactions.

Marcos Almanza came to the United States from Bolivia. He is a construction worker and lives in Arlington, Virginia.

4. I volunteer my time with *Desarrollo Comunal* which helps raise money for our village back home in Bolivia. We do this by having soccer tournaments with teams representing other Bolivian villages. With the money, we have been able to build a water tower, a plaza, and a small clinic. I also volunteer with the American Indian Society of Washington, D.C. I volunteer with them because I am interested in learning about the north side of American Indian culture. Our cultures are similar. Some of my people think it is bad to be an Indian, to speak Quechua or to be Incan. Those kinds of attitudes make me want to show them that it is not bad. I volunteer because I like it. I like to help people. That was the way I was raised. My mother was like that. She used to help a lot of people who came from the mountains. When I see something that I can do, I just say to myself, okay, I will do it.

B. List three facts you remember about each volunteer without looking at the stories. Compare your answers with those of members of your group.

Vlasta Zhang

_____
_____
_____
_____

Chiyo Yasuda

_____
_____
_____
_____

Steve Barrigar

_____
_____
_____
_____

Marcos Almanza

_____
_____
_____
_____

Japan is an island nation located east of Korea surrounded by the Sea of Japan and the Pacific Ocean. More than 125,000,000 people live there. It is called the "Land of the Rising Sun" and its flag shows a red sun on a white background. Japan has one of the most powerful economies in the world and is a leader in technology.

78 •••   ••• 79

INSTRUCTOR'S JOURNAL

_____

_____

_____

_____

_____

_____

_____

| Page 78 | Correlates with: | Page 79 |

Workbook: pages 62–63
Activity Masters: page 57

AUTHORS' NOTES ● ● ●

After they have listened to each other's story, they must then reflect on what they have learned from their classmates and write the facts they remember.

Learners can write comprehension questions for the different volunteers as an extended activity. Have them write one question for each volunteer. Choose one student to read one of her questions aloud for the class. After she reads her question, she can call on a classmate to answer the question. The class can decide if it is answered correctly. In this way, learners practice writing, speaking, and listening.

FIELD TESTERS' NOTES ● ● ●

To help with the retelling of the story, I told them to summarize the information about the four volunteers: talk about where they are from, what kind of volunteer work they do, why they like it, etc. As a follow up I asked:

- *Generally, why do you think people do volunteer work?*
- *Would you ever do volunteer work? Why or why not?*
- *If you were going to do volunteer work, what kind of work would you do?*
- *Of the different people you have learned about, which one do you admire most? Why?*
- *Of the different kinds of volunteer work you have learned about, which kinds do you think you could do? Which would you not like to do?*

Marge Matoba
Fremont Adult School
Sacramento, CA

8 Ideas for Action: Getting Information

A. Several countries are mentioned in the stories of the volunteers. Can you locate the countries on a map?

B. What do you know about these countries? What would you like to know? Where can you get more information? Complete the table below.

Country	I already know	I want to know	Sources for information
Croatia			
Bosnia			
Japan			
Somalia			
Togo			
Bolivia			

C. Use your list of sources and get information about one country.

D. Report your information to the class.

Learning Strategy

When giving a written or oral report, choose a topic that interests you and keep it short and specific. Don't try to answer too many questions at one time.

 9 Bringing the Outside In: Asking Questions

Choose **one** of the following with your class.

1. Take a poll with your class, decide on a topic, and write a question about the topic. Ask friends, co-workers and family members their opinions. Bring your results to class. Make a table graph showing the results.

2. Interview someone who does volunteer work. Before doing the interview, brainstorm with your class to get ideas for questions you could ask. Share your information with the class.

 10 Doing It in English: Offering to Do Something

A. People offer to do something in many different ways. Brainstorm with the class. Can you think of expressions you have heard people use when offering, accepting, or declining help?

List as many as you can.

_____
_____
_____
_____
_____

B. Work with a partner to create conversations for the following situations. Show the class.

Example
A woman is talking to her friend on the telephone.

WOMAN: *I fell off a ladder and broke a bone in my foot. I have to wear the cast for six weeks.*

FRIEND: *Can I help you with anything?*

WOMAN: *Would you mind getting me a few things at the grocery store?*

FRIEND: *I'd be happy to. What do you need?*

WOMAN: *Just some milk, coffee, and bananas. Thanks so much!*

Thank you!
Spanish: *Gracias*
Croatian: *Hvala*
Mina (Togo): *Apke*

Somalia is the easternmost country on the African continent. The capital is Mogadishu. Most of Somalia lies on a plateau. It is cooler and has more rainfall there than on the coast along the Indian Ocean. In general, the climate is hot and dry. Recent civil conflict has caused many Somalies to flee their country to neighboring countries, Europe, and the United States.

INSTRUCTOR'S JOURNAL

AUTHORS' NOTES • • •

8 This activity builds on the previous one by referring to the countries mentioned in the jigsaw readings. Learners evaluate their knowledge on a subject and then gather information they are interested in learning more about. To facilitate their research work, a field trip to the local library would be very useful. Also have learners identify three possible resources for information. These resources can be anything—from the Internet to a fellow classmate.

The outline exercise in the *Workbook* can help learners organize their information before they report it to the class. The reporting can be done either in writing or orally depending on what you think would be most beneficial to your class. Writing an essay or giving a short speech will help students develop academic skills.

9 This activity provides learners with another opportunity to gather information independently and report back to the class. It is a chance for them to practice wh- questions and talk to people in their community. Learners may need help in finding volunteers to interview. If they choose this topic, we suggest they also do the "Options for Learning" activity, *Identifying Volunteer Opportunities in the Community.* Through this activity, learners can identify places in their community where they can meet volunteers.

10 The opposite of asking for help is offering help. Learners may already have a repertoire of expressions they have heard or used. Brainstorm what they already know and be prepared to fill in the gaps. Common expressions of offering help include:

Can ⎫
May ⎭ I help you } with . . . + verb
Let me give you a hand.
Need any help?
Would you like me to . . .

FIELD TESTERS' NOTES • • •

10 *The brainstorming for the activity was very fruitful and showed that some students have a high level of conversational sophistication. After we read the sample dialogue, I had students pair off, choose one of the situations, write a dialogue, practice it, and present it in front of the class. I neglected to say that they should learn the dialogue sufficiently that they would not need their papers. Next time, I would emphasize that.*

Gayle Roby
Bunker Hill Community College
Charlestown, MA

Scene: Two strangers meet in a parking lot.

_____
_____
_____
_____
_____
_____
_____
_____

Scene: Two students are studying together.

_____
_____
_____
_____
_____
_____
_____

The Republic of Croatia gained independence from Yugoslavia on June 25, 1991. It shares a border with Hungary, and the now independent states of Bosnia and Herzegovina, Serbia, Montenegro, and Slovenia. The Adriatic Sea borders Croatia in the east. The capital is Zagreb, an historic city with architecture dating back to the fifteenth century. Croatia is an important industrial and mining center, but the political instability in the region has caused economic and political problems.

 Options for Learning: English in the Community

A. How do you want to get information about your local community services? How do you want to practice English in your community? Check (✔) your answers. Add others if you wish.

	Already Do	Want to Learn	Not Interested
Locate information about community services from the telephone book	_____	_____	_____
Call for information about community services	_____	_____	_____
Identify opportunities to volunteer in your community	_____	_____	_____
Locate community places on a map	_____	_____	_____
Other? _____	_____	_____	_____

B. Tell a partner or the class what you already do and what you want to learn.

C. Ask your teacher for a *Collaborations* worksheet to work on one of these goals.

 Looking Back

Think about your learning. Complete this form. Then tell the class your ideas.

A. The most useful thing I learned in this unit was _____
_____.

B. I would still like to learn _____.

C. I learned the most by working
_____ alone. _____ with a partner. _____ with a group.

D. The activity I liked best was 1 2 3 4 5 6 7 8 9 10 11
because _____.

E. The activity I liked least was 1 2 3 4 5 6 7 8 9 10 11
because _____.

INSTRUCTOR'S JOURNAL

_____

_____

_____

_____

_____

_____

_____

Page 82	Correlates with:	Page 83
		Activity Masters: pages 55–58

AUTHORS' NOTES ● ● ●

10 For an extended activity, give the learners a situation to improvise in a role play. Possible situations are:

- An old man or woman carrying a heavy suitcase
- A co-worker drops files with papers or several boxes
- Someone is lost and looking at a map

Another activity that would tie into the "Learning Log" in the *Workbook* would be to have the learners watch a television show and record if and when they heard offers, acceptances, or refusals of help.

11 The "Options for Learning" activity provides students with opportunities to identify and gather information about their community independently. It is helpful if they work in pairs on these activities. For further suggestions, see Unit 1, page 17.

12 See Unit 1, page 17 for an explanation of "Looking Back."

FIELD TESTERS' NOTES ● ● ●

12 *I was surprised by the diversity of opinions. The tastes of students and what they feel they need vary greatly.*

Gayle Roby
Bunker Hill Community College
Charlestown, MA

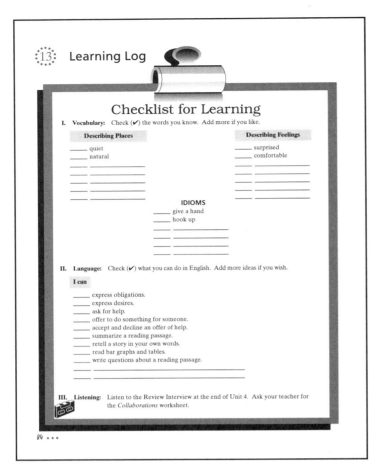

AUTHORS' NOTES • • •

13 Learners look back on their work in this unit and assess their accomplishments. The checklist gives them a visual record of what they have done and what they need to work on more. You might want them to share their Checklists with a partner and explain their entries.

INSTRUCTOR'S JOURNAL

Page 84	Correlates with:
Workbook: pages 65–66 **Activity Masters: page 59** **Audiotape: Review Interview**	

Staying in Touch Stories from Laos and California

Laos is a small country located in Southeast Asia between Thailand and Vietnam with a population of approximately 4,440,000. The capital of Laos is Vientiane, which is located on the banks of the Mekong River. More than half of the population of Laos is made up of ethnic minorities living in the remote mountainous regions of the country. These groups include the Hmong, Mien, Yao, and Khmu.

California

Los Angeles is located on the coast of southern California, on the Pacific Ocean. With a population of approximately 3,485,000, Los Angeles is the second largest city in the United States. The people of Los Angeles are ethnically diverse, with rapidly growing Korean, Mexican, and Southeast Asian immigrant communities. Los Angeles is the center of the entertainment industry and the home of many famous movie and television stars.

The Dengvilay Family Story

A. Look at the photos on this page and the next page. How are the people in the photos alike? How are they different? Discuss the similarities and differences with your classmates before you read the stories.

PART 1: Luang Prabang, Lao People's Democratic Republic

All of our children are grown now. Five of them live in America, and five still live in Laos. One of our daughters spent six years studying in Russia. The two youngest are not married yet, so they still live with us in Luang Prabang. Our oldest daughter is married to a Japanese man who owns a Sushi restaurant in Los Angeles, California. The seventh one lives in Los Angeles, too, with her husband and two young children. We feel very happy whenever we hear from them. They write letters and send us pictures of our new grandchildren.

Mr. Dengvilay owns a furniture shop in Luang Prabang, Laos. Keo Phovilaichit lives in Sydney, Australia. In this photo, he is translating a letter from Mr. Dengvilay's granddaughter.

We Lao people love our families very much. Not a day goes by that I don't think about our children, even if they are halfway around the world. Of course, they write us letters in Lao, but our grandchildren can write only in English.

This letter arrived about six months ago from our granddaughter in Texas, but we weren't able to read it for a long time. We can speak French quite well, but not a word of English.

A few days ago, our neighbor's son came home for a visit. He lives in Australia now. He said he would be happy to translate the letter for us.

In Laos, we take care of our parents when they get very old. My mother still lives with us. Everyone here calls her Grandmother Pheng. She is 95 years old, but she is still in good health. She was married to a Frenchman, but he died when I was a young boy. She never told me much about my father, but I know she remembers him. She helped raise most of our children because my wife and I were so busy in those days.

After 1975, life became very hard for us here in Laos. That's why five of our children decided to leave. We worried about them night and day. We were really upset when we heard that our oldest daughter got robbed! Last year was a lucky year for us because two of our daughters came back to Laos to visit us. We hadn't seen them for more than ten years. How grown up and successful they looked! We hope that the others will be able to come home someday, too.

Mr. Dengvilay's youngest son, Saisana, with Grandmother Pheng.

PART 2: Los Angeles, California

Four of Mr. Dengvilay's grown children gather at Bouakham's home in Los Angeles. From left: Bouaket, Bouachan, Bounthavy, and Bouakham.

Bouachan's Story

In Laos, I was a teacher. I used to be fluent in French, but I've forgotten most of it now. Here in America, I'm a business person. I run a Sushi restaurant in Los Angeles with my husband. He's Japanese. Life is pretty good here most of the time, but I miss my parents and friends in Laos. I wish we could all be together. I'm very close to my sisters and brothers, and I'm glad that we live in the same area so we can visit each other often.

The worst thing that happened to me was when I got robbed a few years ago. I had just come back from work and opened the door to my bedroom. Then this guy jumped out. He told me to lie down on the floor and he put a towel over me.

I told him, "Go ahead, take anything you want, but don't hurt me."

He told me not to move until he said it was OK. Then I waited. I was too scared to do anything. I kept waiting, but still he didn't say anything. Nothing happened. Finally, I asked him, "Hey! Are you OK?"

There was no answer, so I turned my head and looked up. He was gone, and so was everything else except my wedding ring! Still, it was a close call. I'm happy that I didn't get hurt. I was lucky. It could have been much worse. It's better to lose everything as long as you keep your life.

In Laos, most people think it's easy to get rich in America. They don't know how hard it is. I may go back to live in Laos someday, but probably not until I get a lot older. Then maybe I'll want to go back for good. If I went back now, I'd have to start all over again.

Next year, we are planning to bring our parents to California for a visit, just for a couple of months. I don't think my mom would want to stay here forever, though. She enjoys spending a lot of time at the temple with her friends. That's the way most of the older ladies in Luang Prabang spend their time, getting ready to pass on to the next life. It wouldn't be easy for her to do that here.

> **IDIOMS**
> for good
> pass on
> close call

- What do you remember best about your country?
- How do you stay in touch with your family and friends back home?
- Do you ever plan to return? When?
- Have you ever had a close call? What happened? What did you learn from it?

INSTRUCTOR'S JOURNAL

Page 85	Correlates with:	Page 86
Transparency: page 17		Audiotape: Story on tape
Audiotape: Story on tape		Workbook: pages 00 and 00

86 • • •

AUTHORS' NOTES • • •

In this unit, we took the risk of presenting stories based in two of the lesser known areas of the world with the intention of encouraging learners, wherever they are from, to become resources on their countries and cultures of origin. It is likely that adults from around the world will find parallels from their own experiences in the stories of the Dengvilay (pronounced DENG-vee-lai) family, particularly in their persistence in maintaining close family relationships across thousands of miles.

The photographs on the opening page may well bring back memories of how it felt to arrive in North America, and of the contrast between the industrialized and developing parts of the world. You may want to touch on this contrast in the opening discussion, then show the transparency, or have learners look at the photographs on pages 86 and 87. Points for discussion include the changes people go through when they move into completely new environments and ways of staying in touch with family and friends back home. What are some of the difficulties in maintaining communication across international boundaries?

1 Part 1: As one way of approaching these stories, you may want to have half of the class read the story from Luang Prabang (pronounced LOO-ahng-pra-bahng) and the other half read the story from Los Angeles, as happened in Diane Satin's class. Learners can then pair off and tell each other what happens in each.

Part 2: Bouachan's (pronounced Boo-ah-CHAN) personal narrative, which was told to us in a rather bemused yet relieved tone at a family gathering in Los Angeles, includes a survival story which she clearly hoped would serve as advice to other victims of crime.

The last discussion question may spark stories similar to Bouachan's, since few immigrants are immune from such experiences. We urge caution in letting learners give as many or as few details they as wish to reveal to the class, and reminding them that they may prefer to relate these stories in their journals.

FIELD TESTERS' NOTES • • •

I had students locate their own countries on a world map and show others. Some stayed in their seats, and others went around the class.

We discussed similarities and differences between Laos and Los Angeles, California—Laos is smaller, LA is a city, Laos is a country, Laos is more rural, LA is an urban area and so on.

Diana Satin
Jamaica Plain Learning Program
Jamaica Plain, MA

1 *Students got into two groups, one of five and the other of six. Group one read the story from Laos, and group two read the story from Los Angeles. Some people discussed their own articles and asked about each other's. I asked each group to make up several questions about the story they read. They wrote their questions on the board. Then one group read their story aloud, while the other listened for answers to the questions. They were anxious to correct the grammar and spelling of their questions, but with our limited time that day, I said we'd make the corrections next class, and we would concentrate on answering the questions that night.*

Diana Satin
Jamaica Plain Learning Program
Jamaica Plain, MA

2 Sharing Ideas: Story Reactions

A. The Dengvilay Family Story was told by two people: Mr. Dengvilay in Laos, and his eldest daughter, Bouachan, in Los Angeles. Use the information below to help you remember each part. Then take turns retelling the parts of story from each person's point of view.

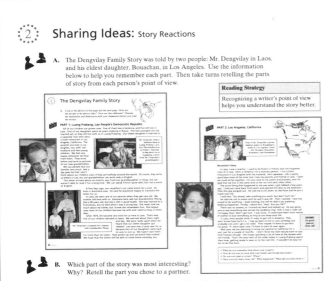

Reading Strategy

Recognizing a writer's point of view helps you understand the story better.

B. Which part of the story was most interesting? Why? Retell the part you chose to a partner.

C. Do you have anything in common with the Dengvilay family? Check the sentences from the story that are also true for you. Discuss your responses with the whole class.

	True for me	Not true for me
Not a day goes by when I don't think about our children.	❑	❑
We take care of our parents when they get very old.	❑	❑
Last year was a lucky year.	❑	❑
Life is pretty good here most of the time.	❑	❑
Maybe when I get a lot older, I'll want to go back for good.	❑	❑
It's better to lose everything as long as you keep your life.	❑	❑

3 Playing with Story Language

A. A storyboard is a sequence of pictures and words used to plan movies and television dramas. Listen again as Bouachan tells the story of the robbery. Think about how this story might be made into a storyboard.

B. Rewrite the scene of the robbery in the form of a storyboard. Imagine that your storyboard will be used to produce an action packed movie or television show. Write the words you think Bouachan and the robber said or thought on the lines below each picture.

C. Share your storyboard dialogues with another set of partners. How is this scene similar to scenes you have seen in a movie or on TV? What did Bouachan learn from her experience? Why is it often helpful for victims of crimes such as these to share their stories with others?

INSTRUCTOR'S JOURNAL

Page 88	Correlates with:	Page 89
Workbook: pages 71–72		

AUTHORS' NOTES ● ● ●

2   This activity introduces the concept of "point of view" in storytelling, and asks students to recall the main points from both perspectives without turning back to the stories themselves. It may be helpful to jog learners' memories using prompts such as:

> *Where does the elder Mr. Dengvilay live?*
> *Why is he standing next to the man from*
>   *Australia?*
> *How is the woman in the right picture related to*
>   *Mr. Dengvilay?*
> *Why was he worried about her?*

You may want to take this opportunity to further define the concept of "point of view" in writing by calling attention to the Reading Strategy box and asking students whose point of view each story is told from. Ask them to turn back to the story and refer to evidence of this (such as the use of first person "I"). Then have them look back at the introductory descriptions of Laos and Los Angeles on the opening page. How is the point of view on this page different? (It is external and objective.)

3   **A.–B.** We have found the use of storyboards especially helpful for students who can both comprehend and express themselves better by "thinking in pictures." The drawings are intended to help visualize what went on during the robbery incident related by Bouachan and to "play with story language" by translating from personal narrative to dramatic reconstruction of dialogue.

   C. Before students begin this small group discussion, you might mention that storyboards are used to plan television and movie dramas. Since the questions posed here are purposefully open, we suggest that you let the discussion in each group go where it will while you "eavesdrop" for a while on each group, taking note of the issues and opinions that arise. As a follow-up, you may simply want to ask the groups what they learned from the discussion.

FIELD TESTERS' NOTES ● ● ●

2   *Before we began, I reintroduced the story questions the students had written the first day. It struck me as interesting that the questions they had generated actually reflected their own interests and concerns.*

> Diana Satin
> Jamaica Plain Learning Program
> Jamaica Plain, MA

   C. *This activity encouraged the students to interact with the text.*

> Mary K. Shea
> ESL Adult Education Teacher
> Annandale, VA

3   *I found it important to make sure students understood what a storyboard is. Most of my students didn't know.*

> Mary K. Shea
> ESL Adult Education Teacher
> Annandale, VA

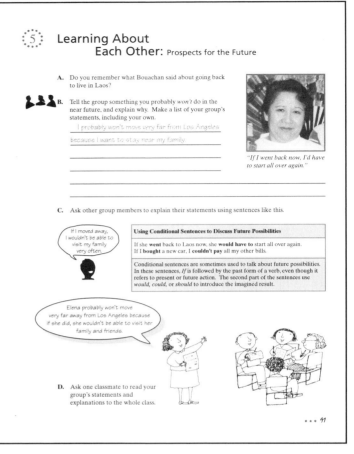

4 Sharing Experiences: Imagining What We Would Have Done

A. Think about Bouachan's experience and how she felt after it was over.

"I'm happy that I didn't get hurt. I was lucky. It could have been much worse. It's better to lose everything as long as you keep your life."

B. Get together with a small group of your classmates. Discuss what you would have done in her place.

> I would have tried to run away.

> Not me. I would have done exactly what she did.

Bouachan Dengvilay with her sister and niece at the Thai Buddhist temple in Los Angeles.

> I'm not sure. I might have tried to call the police.

Using Conditional Sentences to Talk About Past Possibilities

She **could have tried** to get his gun away.
I **would have given** him all my money.

Past conditional sentences describe past situations in which the facts are changed. In these types of sentences, the main subject is followed by a modal (*would, could, might*) + have + the past participle form of the verb.

C. Tell the group about a close call or another interesting thing that happened to you. Explain what you learned from the experience. Invite the members of your group to tell what they would have done in your shoes.

IDIOM
in (someone else's) shoes

D. In the space below, summarize one of your classmate's stories. Tell briefly what happened, what he or she learned, and what you would have done.

Example: Suhair got lost in downtown Los Angeles late at night. She asked a

policeman for help. I would have done exactly the same thing.

5 Learning About Each Other: Prospects for the Future

A. Do you remember what Bouachan said about going back to live in Laos?

B. Tell the group something you probably *won't* do in the near future, and explain why. Make a list of your group's statements, including your own.

I probably won't move very far from Los Angeles

because I want to stay near my family.

"If I went back now, I'd have to start all over again."

C. Ask other group members to explain their statements using sentences like this.

> If I moved away, I wouldn't be able to visit my family very often.

Using Conditional Sentences to Discuss Future Possibilities

If she **went** back to Laos now, she **would have to** start all over again.
If I **bought** a new car, I **couldn't pay** all my other bills.

Conditional sentences are sometimes used to talk about future possibilities. In these sentences, *If* is followed by the past form of a verb, even though it refers to present or future action. The second part of the sentences use *would, could,* or *should* to introduce the imagined result.

> Elena probably won't move very far away from Los Angeles because if she did, she wouldn't be able to visit her family and friends.

D. Ask one classmate to read your group's statements and explanations to the whole class.

INSTRUCTOR'S JOURNAL

Page 90	Correlates with:	Page 91
Workbook: page 73		

AUTHORS' NOTES • • •

4   Although the activities on this page have a grammatical focus, they also extend the discussion of Bouachan's story by asking learners to put themselves in her shoes. We have found this to be such an engaging exchange that students often forget that they are actually using a complex grammatical form in the process! As with other activities that incorporate explanatory boxes, we suggest that students perform the communicative activity prior to focusing on the formal explanation.

As your group might notice, Bouachan's chosen course of action and philosophy reflect a typically Southeast Asian perspective on dealing with difficult situations, that is, following the path of least resistance. During the class interaction, you might take note of the different cultural perspectives that are expressed, and ask students to reflect on these in their journals or as a follow-up discussion.

5   Students are again asked to speculate, this time about their own lives with the focus on the future, rather than on the past.

B. As a first step, students are invited to make definite statements about what they believe won't happen in the future. These lists set the stage for more complex statements using *if*-clauses with conditional verbs.

C. Learners may need some guidance in orchestrating the transition to more complex statements. If so, it may be helpful to model the exchange, using a statement volunteered by one of the groups. Alternatively, offer a statement of your own, for example:

> *I probably won't go straight home after class.*
> (Invite students to ask you why not)
> *Because if I did, . . .*

Activities that call for students to generate written sentences bring up the issue of how to correct grammatical errors in an upbeat way. We admire the technique Diana Satin uses to turn this into an engaging and enjoyable exercise.

FIELD TESTERS' NOTES • • •

C. When the groups reported their sentences, we had a "sentence auction." I put their sentences on the board and they bid with "$10" paper clips for sentences they thought were grammatically correct. Then we went through each sentence, and I asked them to offer corrections. If they got stuck, I told them how many errors to look for.

Diana Satin
Jamaica Plain Learning Program
Jamaica Plain, MA

⑥ Doing It in English: Expressing Wishes

A. If you had three wishes, what would they be? Read Bouakham's answer.

*First, I wish I could go back home
to visit my grandmother again.
And I wish my children could come
with me so they could see where we
are from. My third wish is one for
the whole world—I wish there
would never be another war.*

Bouakham Dengvilay is Bouachan's younger
sister. She immigrated to the United States
in 1981. Today, she lives in Los Angeles with
her husband and two small children.

B. Tell a partner about three wishes *you* have.
Make a "wish list" for you and your partner.

Expressing Wishes
I wish I **knew** the answer. We wish we all **could be** together again. He wishes he **were** rich and famous.
To express a wish in the present or future time, use the past plural form of a verb, even if the subject is singular. You can also use a modal such as *could* or *would* + a basic verb form.

Our Wish List
1. *We wish we had
more time to study.*
2. *We wish we had
more money.*

⑦ Journal Writing

Some people wish for things that cannot possibly come true, while
others make more realistic wishes. What do you wish for most often?
Why do you wish for it? What are the chances of it coming true? Let
your imagination fly. Write about one or more of your favorite wishes.

⑧ Think It Over: Learning from History

A. The article describes a recent event and summarizes the history of
modern Laos. Before you read, scan the article for the following
information.

Year of Lao independence from France: _____

Name of the country after 1975: _____

Number of refugees who left Laos: _____

Reading Strategy
When you *scan* an article for specific facts, look only for the information you want to find. Then read the article to get the whole picture.

A Bridge to Peace

In its glory, Laos was known as "The Kingdom of a Million Elephants and of the White Parasol." In modern Laos, elephants have become a rare sight, and busloads of foreign tourists line up outside the gates of the former royal palace. After nearly twenty years of isolation from much of the world, with its economy at a virtual standstill, the country's leaders have taken the first cautious steps toward the twenty-first century. With the completion of the *Mithapap* (Friendship) Bridge in 1994, which connects Laos with a former enemy, the King of Thailand and the President of the Lao PDR (People's Democratic Republic) joined hands to symbolize the beginning of a new era.

Given the recent history of this tiny Southeast Asian nation, its leaders have every reason to be cautious. The country has periodically fallen under the domination of its more powerful neighbors, and was a French colony from 1893 to 1953. In 1944, a group of Lao patriots formed the *Lao Issara* (Free Laos) resistance movement. Supported by the international Communist movement, this group later became known as the *Pathet Lao*. Following the French departure from Southeast Asia in 1954, the *Pathet Lao* opposed the Lao Royal Government and the United States involvement in Southeast Asia.

The Mithapap (Friendship) Bridge was completed in 1994.

INSTRUCTOR'S JOURNAL

Page 92	Correlates with:	Page 93
Workbook: page 74		Activity Master: page 68

AUTHORS' NOTES • • •

6   **A.–B.** The "Wish List" activity creates the context for students to use another complex verb form that frequently confuses second language learners. If your students need further practice with subjunctive verbs, we suggest extending the practice using *Workbook* page 00. You could also conduct a whole-class session in which partners volunteer to read their lists aloud, then respond to follow up questions, for example:

> *We wish we could travel around the world.*
> *Why? What places would you see?*
> *If we could travel around the world, we would stop*
>   *in every country and learn more about it.*

7   If it is appropriate for your group of learners, you might want to help spark their imaginations by introducing them to one of the many popular songs and poems that express visions of a better world. Examples include *Imagine, Last Night I Had the Strangest Dream, If I Had a Hammer,* or *From a Distance,* to name a few. Individual writers might even choose one of these to react to in their journals.

8   If your students are unfamiliar with Southeast Asia, it is important to reintroduce them to the region by pointing it out on a world map before asking them to read the magazine article, "A Bridge to Peace." Show the locations of Laos, Cambodia, and Vietnam and point out that all three countries were involved in a long devastating war, which officially ended in 1975. Then have learners look at the photograph and read the caption, then discuss the title.

Before students actually begin to read the article, introduce the strategy of looking for specific information by scanning the whole article (which continues onto page 94). If students are unfamiliar with this strategy, you might want to search for the first answer together, noting that looking for a particular type of information, such as a number, a date, or a capitalized term, can speed up the search significantly. You could also discuss situations in which readers might use the scanning strategy rather than (or in addition to) reading for ideas and general information.

FIELD TESTERS' NOTES • • •

Although Laos struggled to remain neutral throughout the 1960s, the fighting between the Pathet Lao and the U.S.-backed Royal Government finally erupted into a full-scale civil war. The United States never officially entered the war in Laos, but instead carried on a "secret war," unknown to the American public. As part of this effort, U.S. military personnel provided equipment and training for Hmong fighters from the mountainous regions of the country to oppose the *Pathet Lao*. During this period American planes dropped more than two million tons of bombs over areas of the country that were under Communist control, causing immense destruction and loss of life.

When the United States pulled out of Vietnam in 1975, the King of Laos was forced to abdicate,[1] and the Lao PDR took control of the country, virtually shutting its doors to the West. Fearing reprisals, more than 400,000 refugees fled across the Mekong to camps in Thailand, and eventually to new homes in Western countries.

Laos has received substantial economic aid from Vietnam and the Eastern European countries, yet its per capita income[2] remained one of the lowest in the world. In 1989, when socialism began to collapse in Europe, the Lao leadership had begun to seek more aid and investment from the West. The *Mithapap* Bridge, jointly funded by Thailand, Australia, and Sweden, was built to help stimulate economic growth and promote friendly relations between Laos and Thailand, as well as with the rest of the world. In the meantime, the Lao government has also opened its doors to tourists and to former refugees wishing to return home. Since 1990, thousands of overseas Lao, who are now citizens of other countries, have returned to visit their families. Many have even invested in businesses and contributed to private development projects in their hometowns and villages.

[1] abdicate—to give up ruling power
[2] per capita income—(Latin) average income for each person

Keo Phovilaichit, standing on the right in this photo, works in an automobile factory in Sydney, Australia. He has returned to his hometown of Luang Prabang, the former royal capital of Laos, to visit his mother. When he saves enough money, Keo would like to start a business in Laos. Mr. Vilavong, on the left, is a weaver who sells baskets to tourists in Luang Prabang.

B. Reread the article carefully. Then discuss it with a small group of your classmates, using the questions below as a guide.

Learning Strategy

Discussing your reactions to a reading and identifying related issues can help you express your ideas more clearly.

• Why do you think the present leaders of Laos are cautious about establishing new relations with other countries?
• Name the two most interesting things you learned from this article.
• What other world events (past or present) are you concerned about? Make a list for further discussion.

C. The timeline below shows how events in Laos led up to war and the departure of more than 400,000 refugees. As you read over the timeline, use the map to help you locate key places.

1944	Formation of *Lao Issara* (Free Laos)
1953	Kingdom of Laos receives official independence from France
1954	French departure from Southeast Asia
1954–1957	*Pathet Lao* (Communist movement) gains influence in Laos
1957	Neutralist government established in Vientiane
1961	Agreements break down, U.S. "secret war" in Laos begins
1961–1975	Full scale civil war, backed by the United States and North Vietnam
1975	United States withdraws from Vietnam
1975	Lao People's Democratic Republic established
1975–83	400,000 refugees leave Laos for Thai border camps
1994	*Mithapap* (Friendship) Bridge completed

Learning Strategy

A **timeline** is a list of events in *chronological* order (the order in which they happened). A timeline based on a reading about history can help you understand the whole picture and recall important details.

The three-headed elephant, symbol of the former Kingdom of Laos, and the flag of the Lao PDR at the entrance to the National Museum.

D. Without looking back at the article, practice explaining the events in the timeline to a partner. Use the map and the photo on this page as you discuss events on the timeline. Then discuss these questions.

• What period of history does the timeline cover?
• What was going on in other parts of the world during the same period? List as many events as you can.

INSTRUCTOR'S JOURNAL

Page 94	Correlates with:	Page 95
Transparency: page 18		Activity Master: page 70
Workbook: page 75		

AUTHORS' NOTES ● ● ●

After they complete the scanning exercise, ask students to look at the photograph beneath the article. After they read the caption silently, you could ask students to list the similarities and differences between the two men in the photo. You could also mention that at the time the photo was taken, the Lao government had only recently (since 1993) allowed former refugees to visit Laos without major restrictions. Ask students why they think they were denied permission to visit their families in Laos for so long (18 years), and why the Lao government is now changing its policies.

B. Reading the magazine article in detail is likely to present a major challenge to students who have not encountered texts written in a journalistic style using a relatively sophisticated level of vocabulary. Encourage students to read the article silently first, making notes or marking the terms they do not understand. Then ask them to identify the main topic (the bridge) and give a brief synopsis of each paragraph prior to returning to the text to help students clarify the meaning of new terms.

In the group discussion that follows, make sure learners have adequate time to prepare a list of world events for further discussion. This helps the class make the transfer from concentrating on one area of the world to practicing new language skills and learning strategies in contexts more closely aligned with their own experiences and concerns.

C. You may want to show the class additional graphic representations of timelines as you discuss the example about Laos. Ask students where they might find timelines (history text books, television documentaries) that summarize events in chronological order.

D. Prior to 1975, the Lao National Museum in Luang Prabang was the home of the royal family, most of whom are currently living in exile. However, tourists who visit the museum today, including overseas Lao, are amazed to find all of the former king's belongings—including a moon rock presented by former President Nixon—with government tour guides providing detailed commentary on each display. If you feel this background information will be of interest to your students, you may want to pass it along as they discuss the photograph and the caption.

FIELD TESTERS' NOTES ● ● ●

8 *C. This is a challenging, yet very stimulating activity. Students can follow the same format (the timeline) to organize information and discuss other world issues students are concerned about.*

Mary K. Shea
ESL Adult Education Teacher
Annandale, VA

E. The tapestry in this photograph uses images, rather than words, to tell a story. Use the images in the tapestry to retell the story to a partner. Write your version of the story and read it aloud to another set of partners. Compare your different versions.

Hmong child in Luang Prabang, Laos (1971)

This tapestry was made by Hmong refugee women living in Minnesota. The Hmong are a minority people from the mountainous regions of northern Laos who speak their own language and have their own customs. Since 1975, approximately 100,000 Hmong have settled in communities across North America.

---

 9 **Learning About Each Other:** Major Events

A. Think about an important event in your life. Write notes about the event on the left side of the experience chart.

> I'll never forget my wedding day.

> When was that? Tell me about it.

B. Work with a partner. Ask about an important event in your partner's life. Take notes on the right side of the chart. Ask more questions about parts you don't understand or when you want further information.

Notes on an Important Event in My Life	Notes on an Important Event in My Partner's Life
Time and place	
What happened?	
How did you feel about it then?	
How do you feel about it now?	
Additional information	

INSTRUCTOR'S JOURNAL

AUTHORS' NOTES ● ● ●

8 **E.** Before beginning this page, it is a good idea to introduce tapestries and other forms of woven or embroidered art. This particular "story cloth" was sold by a Hmong (pronounced MOHNG) entrepreneur at a national TESOL conference, who during the course of our conversation recommended that we read *Tragic Mountains: The Hmong, the Americans, and the Secret Wars for Laos 1942–1992* by Jane Hamilton-Merritt (Indiana University Press, 1993). This book provides a detailed account of the U.S. military involvement in Laos, the same story that is told pictorially by the tapestry. The interaction between visual and print literacy, as well as between insider and outsider's views of history struck us as a powerful alliance in the Hmong initiative to have their story heard.

As part of the follow-up discussion, you may want to remind learners of the concept of "point of view" and ask whose point of view the tapestry reflects. If appropriate, mention that a book was written that tells the same story as the tapestry, and ask whose point of view it probably reflects. You might also want to ask what forms of expression are used in learners' own communities to document their recent history, or if they could recommend readings about their own cultures. Examples might include photographs, paintings, videos, songs, poems, posters, oral histories on tape, newspaper articles, and books. Invite learners' explanations on why documenting family and community history is important to them and their children.

Workbook page 76, which gives students practice in recognizing time and sequence clues in discourse, also provides additional historical information about the Hmong.

9 This activity offers students an opportunity to exchange in-depth information about a significant event in their own lives. Allow enough time (about ten minutes) for learners to interview each other in depth. For additional practice with the specific skill of asking for clarification, you may want to use Activity Master 64, either in preparation or as a follow-up to this exercise.

FIELD TESTERS' NOTES ● ● ●

E. If they are interested, students can make their own tapestries to tell stories about (1) family, (2) culture, or (3) self, using collage materials, felt, or other fabrics.
Mary K. Shea
ESL Adult Education Teacher
Annandale, VA

Another Voice from North America

A. Read and enjoy Tsekyi Dolma's story. How does she stay in touch with the past?

Tsekyi Dolma is a registered nurse. She lives in Fullerton, California with her husband and two children.

For over 30 years, I held pictures of Tibet in my memory, as clearly as if it were yesterday. I remember very dim mornings and crossing rivers with shimmering pebbles at the bottom. I went out with my brothers and sisters to tend the sheep and the yaks. We used to catch birds and put a little colored cloth on the wing or neck, then let it go. That way, we could see it flying and say, "this is the bird I caught, and I freed it. This is a sign that no one can kill this bird."

I don't have any memory of when I left Tibet, but I guess I must have been six or seven years old. Our family got separated, and I left Tibet with my mother and my two younger sisters. When we got to Nepal, we found out that the parents had to go to the labor camps, to build roads in India, and the kids were going to be sent to school. We all stood in line, and the parents had to go to one side, and the kids to the other. That is how my sisters and I got separated from our mother, and we never saw her again. She was not used to that kind of life, and they told us that she got lost. That's the only news we heard.

My sisters and I were sent to missionary school in India, and we stayed there for 16 years. We spoke Tibetan among ourselves, but we studied in Hindi. It was only after I got married and came to live in America that I started to improve bit by bit in the Tibetan

IDIOMS
in seventh heaven
package tour
bit by bit
no way

language. I learned to read and write while I was pregnant with my first child.

In 1994, I decided to travel to Tibet. By that time, I had an American passport so I joined a package tour. It was the first time I had been back in more than 30 years. As soon as we landed in Lhasa, I couldn't believe it. Oh! The air was so fresh! I felt like I was in seventh heaven. I ran to the river and drank with my hands, and I never got sick.

About 85–90 percent of the population of Lhasa is now Chinese. It was hard to buy incense or white scarves to offer at the holy places because the shops are all Chinese.

The best part of the whole trip was seeing my relatives, the ones I hadn't seen for over 30 years. They were thrilled. They thought that we were dead, and had been performing special rituals for us each Tibetan New Year. But when I asked them if they would like someday to leave this place and go with us, they said, "no way!"

As for me, I'd love to go back and help Tibetans improve their lives, especially in medical care and education. When Tibet is free, I am sure we will all go back. Right now there are around 100,000 Tibetans in exile, and now we have become educated. We want to go back and build our country.

If you go to Tibet, it might change the way you see the world. I hope to go again, and I encourage all my friends to go, whatever the purpose. The experience will be so tremendous, just like falling in love.

B. What did you learn about Tibet by reading Tsegyi Dolma's story? Write three new pieces of information:

_____

_____

_____

C. Use the information in Tsegyi Dolma's story to complete her personal time line.

D. Think about the major events in your own life. For each event, write down the date and a short note on what happened. Then make your own personal timeline to share with the class.

1959	_____
1960	sent to missionary _____
	_____ graduated from school
1978	qualified as a registered nurse
1980	married Nawang Phuntsog
1982	son, Tenzin, born
1983	immigrated to _____
1986	daughter, Thupten, born
1990	received US citizenship
1994	
1995	moved to California

Tibet is situated on a vast plateau, surrounded by the world's highest mountains. Although Tibet had existed since ancient times as an independent state, it was invaded by Chinese military forces in 1951 and claimed as part of China. A Tibetan rebellion against Chinese rule in 1959 resulted in the flight of the Dalai Lama, the Tibetan spiritual leader, and thousands of his followers to refugee communities in northern India, Great Britain, and the United States. The current population of Tibet is approximately 2,283,000.

Proverbs About Home and Relatives

"Il n'est pire ennemie que ses proches."

Home is where the heart is. (USA)

Water can be diverted in many directions, but blood flows in a single stream. (Laos)

There is no worse enemy than a close relative. (France)

Worry not! Strong winds cannot blow away small pebbles. (Tibet)

INSTRUCTOR'S JOURNAL

Page 98
Audiotape
Workbook: page 77

Correlates with:

Page 99
Workbook: page 78

98 ● ● ●

AUTHORS' NOTES ● ● ●

10 Tsekyi Dolma's (pronounced SIKYI DOLMA) intense feelings for her homeland permeate every line of her narrative, which was related shortly after her return from her first visit to Tibet after 30 years in exile. Like the Hmong, the Tibetan refugee community actively seeks to make its history known to the general public, and despite her busy life in America, Tsekyi was more than willing to devote many hours to relating her personal history, as well as patiently explaining the historical and political context of the Tibetan diaspora.

A. We suggest that you ask students to locate Tibet on the world map (pages vi–vii) and briefly find out what your students already know about this part of the world before they begin to read. To begin, you might try posing such questions as:

What is the capital of Tibet? (Lhasa)
What religion do most Tibetans practice?
   (Buddhism)
Who is the leader of Tibetans in exile? (The Dalai
   Lama)
Why are there Tibetan refugees in India and North
   America? (because of the Chinese occupation)
What else do you know about Tibet?

If one or more of the students in your class are of Chinese origin, we urge you to value any information or opinions they might offer, reminding the class (if necessary) that points of view on any issue may differ, depending on an individual's experience. Judgments about who is "right" and who is "wrong" should only be made after all perspectives have been heard.

Following the introductory discussion, learners should read the whole story silently for general meaning, then complete the request in Part B to write down three things they learned about Tibet. This can provide the basis for further discussion of specific information presented in the story, and remind learners that their own stories can become valuable sources of knowledge. Following the general discussion, you may choose to read the story aloud (or play the tape), then revisit specific terms and idioms that may need further clarification and practice. Keep in mind that having students guess the meaning from context before providing explanations or sending them to their dictionaries is an effective way to build independent reading strategies.

C.–D. In completing Tsekyi's personal timeline and then their own, explain that only key words need be included in the brief descriptions of events. To demonstrate, you might give an example of how a complete sentence *(She was sent to a missionary school in India.)* is reduced to note form.

FIELD TESTERS' NOTES ● ● ●

Bringing the Outside In: News from Home

Bring in a letter from a relative, a videotape, or a recent photograph from relatives or friends in your country. Share it with your classmates. Use maps, posters, or other visual aids that will help your classmates get the picture.

As you listen, take notes on any new information you learned from your classmates' presentations.

I learned that . . .

_____Lhasa is a city in Tibet._____

_____

_____

 ### Ideas for Action: Visit a Travel Agency

A. Plan to telephone or visit a travel agency.

Prepare questions about one or more of the following topics in advance.

1. the cost of a round-trip ticket to a country you would like to visit

2. documents needed for travel to this country (passport, visa, other papers)

3. legal restrictions or other problems for tourists or visitors

4. other helpful information

B. Share what you learned with the class.

 ### Options for Learning: Staying in Touch

A. What do you want to be able to do in English?
Check (✔) your answers. Add other ideas if you wish.

	Already Do	Want to Learn	Not Interested
Plan a travel itinerary			
Write a family history			
Tell a group of Americans about your migration experience			
Read current news articles about events in your home country			
Other?			

 ### Looking Back

Think about your learning. Complete this form. Then tell the class your ideas.

A. The most useful thing I learned in this unit was _____

_____.

B. I would still like to learn _____.

C. I learned the most by working

_____ alone. _____ with a partner. _____ with a group.

D. The activity I liked best was   1   2   3   4   5   6   7   8   9   10   11   12   13

because _____.

E. The activity I liked least was   1   2   3   4   5   6   7   8   9   10   11   12   13

because _____.

INSTRUCTOR'S JOURNAL

_____

_____

_____

_____

_____

_____

_____

_____

_____

Page 100	**Correlates with:**	**Page 101**
Audiotape: Review Interview		**Workbook: pages 79–80**
		Activity Masters: page 71

AUTHORS' NOTES • • •

11 "News from Home" invites learners to share news of their families or friends and teach each other about current events in their home countries. If your class is large, you may want to break the presentation session into small groups. We suggest that you request students to keep their presentations relatively short (five minutes or less) and informal, discouraging them from reading from prepared texts and encouraging interaction between speaker and listeners as much as possible.

12 As with other information-gathering assignments, this activity is best accomplished by learners working in teams of two or three. In many immigrant communities, the best travel "deals" to the home country are available at agencies run by community members themselves. In these cases, encourage your students not only to check with these agencies, but to "shop around" for the best prices and services.

13 The "Options for Learning" activities for this unit offer a range of guided experiences related to the theme of maintaining contacts across distance and time. Each of these is best accomplished with a partner or small group, and one (Tell a group of Americans . . .) requires advance planning to be fully implemented. As in other units, we recommend letting learners choose what they want to learn by completing the questionnaire, then distributing copies of the activities. Learners can then form groups or partnerships according to their interests.

14 Since this is the last opportunity learners will have to "look back," you may want to spend more time than usual on ways learners can establish learning goals and strategies to reach them after they have completed this course. You may want to discuss the concept of life-long learning and to ask them to identify specific goals. In addition, you could ask them to list specific strategies they have developed throughout this level of *Collaborations* that they believe will be most effective in their future learning endeavors.

FIELD TESTERS' NOTES • • •

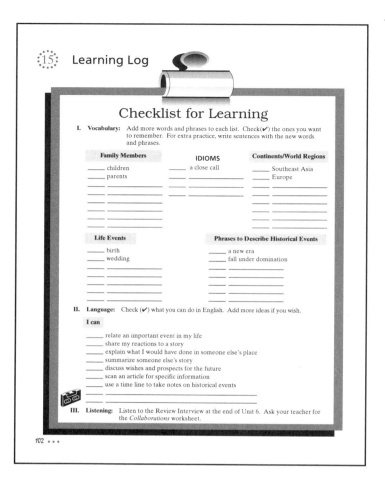

:15: Learning Log

Checklist for Learning

I. Vocabulary: Add more words and phrases to each list. Check(✔) the ones you want to remember. For extra practice, write sentences with the new words and phrases.

Family Members	**IDIOMS**	**Continents/World Regions**
_____ children	_____ a close call	_____ Southeast Asia
_____ parents	_____ _____	_____ Europe
_____	_____ _____	_____ _____
_____	_____ _____	_____ _____
_____		_____ _____
_____		_____ _____

Life Events	**Phrases to Describe Historical Events**
_____ birth	_____ a new era
_____ wedding	_____ fall under domination
_____ _____	_____ _____
_____ _____	_____ _____
_____ _____	_____ _____
_____ _____	_____ _____

II. Language: Check (✔) what you can do in English. Add more ideas if you wish.

I can

_____ relate an important event in my life
_____ share my reactions to a story
_____ explain what I would have done in someone else's place
_____ summarize someone else's story
_____ discuss wishes and prospects for the future
_____ scan an article for specific information
_____ use a time line to take notes on historical events
_____ _____

III. Listening: Listen to the Review Interview at the end of Unit 6. Ask your teacher for the *Collaborations* worksheet.

102 ● ● ●

INSTRUCTOR'S JOURNAL

GLOSSARY OF GRAMMATICAL TERMS

adjective—word that describes a noun or a pronoun: a *beautiful* person, a *peaceful* country, it was *difficult.*

adverb—word that tells us more about a verb, an adjective, or another adverb: I *sometimes* write in English, a *happily* married couple, she sings *extremely* well.

article—word used to mark a noun. In English, there are three articles: *a, an* and *the.*

base form—simplest form of a verb: *see, ask, work.* Also called **simple form.**

clause—group of words containing a subject and a verb, and forming part of a sentence: *Before I came to the United States,* I studied English for just two months.

complement—word or words used after a form of *be* to complete the meaning of the subject. A subject complement is usually an adjective, a noun, or a noun phrase: I've been *hard-working* all my life. I was *an electrical engineer.*

conditional sentence—sentence that states a possibility, usually containing an if clause: *If you go to Tibet,* it might change the way you see the world. *If she went back to Laos now,* she would have to start all over again. *If she had tried to call the police,* the thief might have hurt her.

direct quote—the use of somebody's exact words. In writing, a direct quote is indicated by quotation marks (" "): *"I don't want to go!"* he cried. Also called **direct speech.**

gerund—verb used as a noun; formed by adding *-ing* to the base form of the verb: She doesn't like *working* as a clerk. *Deciding* what to do is difficult sometimes.

indirect question—report of what somebody asked, not using their exact words. Indirect questions do not use questions marks: She wanted to know *when the game would start.*

infinitive—verb form that can function in a sentence as a noun. In English, infinitives are preceded by *to* and do not take endings (-s, -ing, or -ed): He would like *to become* a teacher.

modal—verb used with another (main) verb to add to its meaning. Modals include *can, could, may, must, ought to, will,* and *would.* Also called **modal auxiliary** or **helping verb.**

noun—word used to name a person, place, thing, or idea. My *parents* are originally from northern *India. Sincerity* is really important.

noun phrase—group of words acting together as a noun. He calls himself *a lucky guy.*

object—noun, noun phrase, or noun clause that receives the action of a verb: I had to grind the *corn,* boil the *corn,* and make the *tortillas.* I don't know *what you mean.* An object may also be part of a prepositional phrase: I expected to be living in an *apartment* right away.

passive—verb form that indicates that the subject of the sentence receives the action; passive forms can occur in any tense: The parade *is attended* by thousands of spectators every year; The poem *was written* by Mariano Ramos.

past continuous—verb tense expressing an action that began and ended in the past. Often used in sentences with the simple past to indicate that something was going on at the time another action occurred. She *was taking a bath* when the telephone rang. Also called **past progressive.**

past participle—verb form used mainly in perfect and passive verb phrases. Usually shows past or completed action: has *been,* had *gone,* was *taught.*

past perfect—verb tense expressing an action or situation completed before another action in the past: Maria *had worked* in the factory for several years before she learned to run the business.

past perfect continuous—verb tense expressing an action that continued over a period of time before another action began: They *had been living* in Michigan before they went back to Texas. Also called **past perfect progressive.**

phrasal verb—verb consisting of two words (verb + particle). Phrasal verbs have meanings that are different from the words that make them up, and many are considered idioms: *call up* (telephone), *give in* (surrender), *catch on* (understand).

plural—noun form indicating more than one of a kind; usually formed by adding *-s* or *-es* to the noun: *kids, carrots, peaches.* Some nouns, however, have irregular plurals: *women, people, children;* and some do not take plural forms: *cotton, money, air.*

preposition—word that shows the relationship between a noun and another part of a sentence. Common prepositions include *in, on, around, about, with, for,* and *to.*

preposition cluster—combination of an adjective and a preposition following a form of the verb be: She's *proud of* her children.

prepositional phrase—group of words containing a preposition, a noun, and any additional words used to describe or mark the noun. I'm taking classes *at night.* I need to do something *with my brain.*

present continuous—verb tense that expresses an action that is going on at the present time. Delilah *is working* in her office today. Also called **present progressive.**

present participle—verb form ending in -*ing*; usually used with *be* to show continuous action: They are *living* in Los Angeles now.

present perfect—verb tense that expresses an action or situation that has a strong connection to the present. Often used with *since* and *for:* She *has studied* English for three years (she is still studying it).

pronoun—word that takes the place of a noun, such as *she, him, themselves, my, it.* Most pronouns have different forms, depending on their use in a sentence.

pronoun reference—relationship between a pronoun and the noun it is taking the place of. To indicate this relationship clearly, pronouns are usually close to their nouns. We had nine *kids. They* all worked except the baby.

relative pronoun—words like *that, which,* and *who* that show the relationship of a descriptive clause to a noun in the sentence. I want my poetry to be understood by people *who* have no education at all.

relative clause—the whole clause, beginning with a relative pronoun, that describes the noun it follows. I want to find a job in Atlanta *that fits my personality.*

reported speech—retelling of what somebody said, not using their exact words: She told me *that she had worked in the strawberry fields.* Also called **indirect speech** or **indirect quote.**

simple future—verb tense that expresses expected action or condition in the future. Formed by combining *will* or *am/is/are* + *going to* + base form of the verb.

simple form—basic form of a verb: *see, ask, work.* Also called **base form.**

simple past—verb tense that expresses a single, completed action or situation that happened or was true in the past. Formed by adding -*ed* to a regular verb, or using the irregular past form. Yesterday I *visited* Atlanta and saw many of my people. I *saw* the trees and animals and I *felt* the fresh air and quiet.

simple present—verb tense that expresses an action or situation that is habitual (happens again and again) is true at the present time, or is always true. She *speaks* three languages. Children *are* children.

singular—noun form indicating one of a kind; *bridge, elephant, day*

subject—noun, pronoun, noun phrase, or noun clause that is the doer of the action expressed by the main verb. In English, the subject almost always comes near the beginning of a sentence: *Life* is pretty good here most of the time. *Not a day* goes by when I don't think about our children. *What I want* and *what I must do* are two different things.

subject-verb agreement—necessity for verbs to agree with their subjects within a sentence. In general, a singular or uncountable noun takes a singular verb: *The bride* usually *wears* a white dress; *Education is* the main goal. A plural noun takes a plural verb: My *parents are* originally from northern India.

uncountable noun—noun that represents a whole group or type of item, such as sugar, water, fruit. These nouns do not take plural forms. Also called **noncount** or **mass** nouns.

verb—word that expresses action or existence. My family *moved* here; They *are* students.

wh-question—question beginning with *what, when, where, whose, how,* or *why.* Also called **information question.**

COMMON IRREGULAR VERBS

Base (Present) Form	Past Form	Past Participle
awake	awoke	awoken
be	was, were	been
become	became	become
begin	began	begun
bite	bit	bitten (or bit)
bleed	bled	bled
blow	blew	blown
break	broke	broken
bring	brought	brought
build	built	built
buy	bought	bought
catch	caught	caught
choose	chose	chosen
come	came	come
cost	cost	cost
cut	cut	cut
dig	dug	dug
do	did	done
draw	drew	drawn
drink	drank	drunk
drive	drove	driven
eat	ate	eaten
fall	fell	fallen
feed	fed	fed
feel	felt	felt
fight	fought	fought
find	found	found
fly	flew	flown
forget	forgot	forgotten
forgive	forgave	forgiven
freeze	froze	frozen
get	got	gotten
give	gave	given
go	went	gone
grow	grew	grown
have	had	had
hear	heard	heard
hide	hid	hidden
hit	hit	hit
hold	held	held
hurt	hurt	hurt
keep	kept	kept
know	knew	known
lay	laid	laid
lead	led	led
leave	left	left
lend	lent	lent

Base (Present) Form	Past Form	Past Participle
let	let	let
lie	lay	lain
light	lit	lit
lose	lost	lost
make	made	made
mean	meant	meant
meet	met	met
pay	paid	paid
prove	proved	proven (or proved)
put	put	put
quit	quit	quit
read	read	read
ride	rode	ridden
ring	rang	rung
rise	rose	risen
run	ran	run
say	said	said
see	saw	seen
seek	sought	sought
sell	sold	sold
send	sent	sent
shake	shook	shaken
shine	shone	shone
shoot	shot	shot
shut	shut	shut
sing	sang	sung
sit	sat	sat
sleep	slept	slept
speak	spoke	spoken
spend	spent	spent
stand	stood	stood
steal	stole	stolen
swear	swore	sworn
sweep	swept	swept
swim	swam	swum
take	took	taken
teach	taught	taught
tell	told	told
think	thought	thought
throw	threw	thrown
understand	understood	understood
wake	woke	woken
wear	wore	worn
weep	wept	wept
win	won	won
write	wrote	written

INDEX

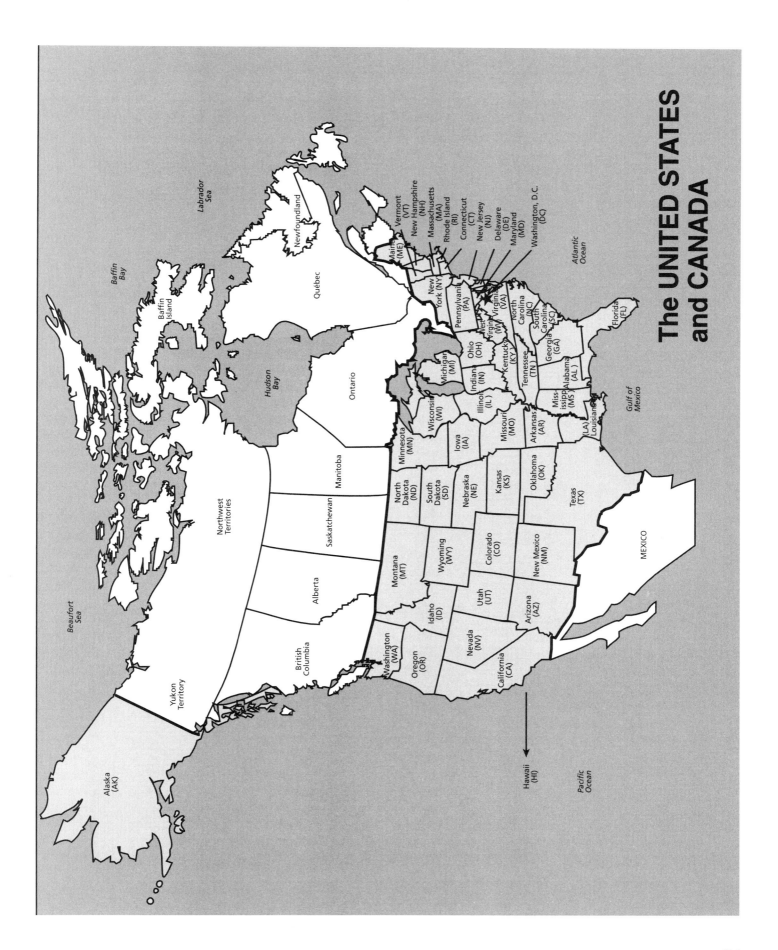

The UNITED STATES
and CANADA